VULTURE CULTURE

VULTURE CULTURE

Dirty Deals, Unpaid Claims, and the
Coming Collapse of the Insurance Industry

ERIC D. GERST

James Edgar
and
Jean Jessop Hervey
Point Loma Branch Library

AMACOM

AMERICAN MANAGEMENT ASSOCIATION

New York • Atlanta • Brussels • Chicago • Mexico City • San Francisco
Shanghai • Tokyo • Toronto • Washington, D.C.

This publication is designed to provide accurate and authoritative information in regard to the subject matter covered. It is sold with the understanding that the publisher is not engaged in rendering legal, accounting, or other professional service. If legal advice or other expert assistance is required, the services of a competent professional person should be sought.

Library of Congress Cataloging-in-Publication Data
  Gerst, Eric D.
    Vulture culture : dirty deals, unpaid claims, and the coming collapse of the insurance industry / Eric D. Gerst.—1st ed.
      p.   cm.
    Includes bibliographical references and index.
    ISBN-13: 978–0-8144–0026–5
    ISBN-10: 0–8144–0026–4
    1. Insurance—Corrupt practices—United States.   2. Insurance law—United States.
  I. Title.
  HG8531.G47   2008
  368.00973—dc22

2007045805

Printing number

10   9   8   7   6   5   4   3   2   1

*To the many thousands of people—policyholders, claimants, insurance
employees, regulators, government employees, healthcare specialists,
business owners and employees, shareholders, professionals, educators,
students, people in good health, ill health and disabled, and the general
public— who, for various reasons, are unable to speak out individually to
change the insurance system in the United States.*
This book is their voice.

CONTENTS

The insurance industry is one of the backbones of the U.S. economy, yet it is now in danger of total collapse. [1] The previously quiet industry has been hit with a perfect storm—a convergence of serious problems that have been building for years and came together at one time with high media coverage. The results have become disastrous for insurer and insured alike.

The problems include rogue executives who put themselves and their shareholders ahead of the policyholders' best interests; insurers who lack sufficient claim reserves to pay claims when a catastrophe arises; an inadequate audit system to monitor insurer practices; and, in some çases, out-and-out reckless conduct or worse on the part of insurers, leaving many innocent claimants, policyholders, and/or employees with nothing when a company is declared insolvent and liquidated.

There are also other troubling issues, such as uncontrolled takeovers of domestic insurers by international or foreign corporations; rapidly increasing general insurance costs and skyrocketing healthcare and medical malpractice premiums; and reckless delay or denial of legitimate claims. There are questionable unregulated offshore reinsurers (reinsurers that take a major part of the risk from primary insurance companies) as well as insurance executives who are convicted of bid rigging, fraud, and conflict of interest, as well as being accused of flat-out greed.

Good management, good executives, and good regulation can save the insurance industry. Regulation may in fact be the ultimate answer to the industry's problems. In 2007, the American Bar Association Tort Trial & Insurance Practice Section identified the move toward federal regulation of the insurance industry—the underlying topic of this book—as one of the current emerging issues for 2005–2007.[1] In this book, I review why problems exist in the industry, what the impact has been on consumers and the industry, and I offer a real solution.

Almost all of us are consumers of insurance. We drive automobiles. We have health problems. We are involved in accidents. We have fires in our houses. We have business disputes. We are sued. We die. For all these and other reasons, we buy insurance to protect us and our families against these possibilities. Almost as important as the monetary protection insurance provides is something equally important: peace of mind. When we buy insurance, we buy a promise for the future—for ourselves, for our loved ones, for our businesses. We trust that at some point in the future, when we need it, the insurance company will be there to pay our legitimate claims, fairly and promptly.

Unfortunately, today's insurance industry has so many problems that your insurance company may not be able to deliver its part of the bargain: the peace of mind and trust that you are paying dearly for. The insurance system, as it exists, offers no reliable protection.

For more than thirty years, I have worked as an attorney. A major part of my practice has been in the insurance field representing corporate and individual clients. I have created and represented insurance businesses. I have drafted insurance policies. I have litigated for both plaintiffs and defendants, negotiated with regulators, and acted as a legal consultant. I was always a firm believer in the positive benefits of insurance for everyone—a necessary part of life. I still believe that. However, I now believe as well that there is something fundamentally wrong with the insurance field.

Several years ago, to my great surprise, my insurance carrier inexplicably turned down an insurance claim I made. I settled the case, but only at substantial financial cost and emotional turmoil. It was then that I decided to take a good hard look at the huge insurance industry (with more than $1.4 trillion in premium volume in 2006, the latest information available from the NAIC). I spent several years researching all aspects of the industry. What I found shocked me and compelled me to write this book.

There is no uniformity in the insurance laws of the various states. Insurance principles may be applied for or against you depending on the state in which you live, the so-called luck of the draw. Consumers of insurance are losing millions of dollars in delayed and denied claim payments in a system favoring the insurer. Insurers, on the other hand, are bombarded with an unworkable fifty-state regulatory system, with each state having its own labyrinth of rules, making the overall system costly, duplicative, and hard to operate within.

The mounting problems have reached a critical mass and have engendered what I call a *vulture culture*—a poorly regulated, uncontrolled business climate where negative forces are allowed to flourish and prey on the unwary. Hundreds of thousands of people have been financially and emotionally hurt in the process, and millions of dollars have been lost, needlessly, by both the insurer and the consumer. This is not to say that all those in the industry are evil; the large majority are not. But the insurance system is in serious disrepair and needs to be fixed, and many in the industry agree.

In *Vulture Culture: Dirty Deals, Unpaid Claims, and the Coming Collapse of the Insurance Industry,* we will examine the many problems that affect the consumer and the insurance industry and review the various options. *Vulture Culture* is written on a number of levels. First, it is a quick-read primer for anyone curious about the current state of the industry. Second, it is a researched and informative guide for management, executives, professionals, educators, legislators, and others who need to be informed about what's going on in this important field.

In my view, the vulture culture has arrived. It needs to be repelled, with a systemic, positive transformation, or it could devour us all. It is in all of our best interests to make sure that the insurance industry is restored to good health.

Vulture Culture sounds the alarm. It can also act as a force for positive change.

Note

1. "Currently Identified Emerging Issues," American Bar Association, Tort Trial & Insurance Practice Section, Emerging Issues Committee, September 2007, www.abanet.org/tips/emerging/issues.html.

ACKNOWLEDGMENTS

Even though I spent my career writing in the legal profession, nothing prepared me for the writing of this book, my first. It required a dedication to the task, constantly being on the alert for new and interesting information, and most of all, to bring across a message that is clear to the reader, whether a layman or professional. I never thought I would be preparing an acknowledgment list, because I was never sure when the book would be finished. In fact the story continues, but the book, for now, is completed.

I want to thank so many people, who in one way or another, were integral parts of bringing this book to life.

Thank you. . . . To my family: my dear wife Carol; children, Jeff and Liz; son-in-law Nick; and granddaughter Emma—all have given me inspiration, good ideas, and love.

To the rest of my immediate family, and my extended family—who encouraged me to move forward, to put my words and observations into book form.

To my friends—old and new, including my tennis buddies, who believed in my message.

To my professional colleagues, who put a calculating, learned eye toward the text.

To my researchers and staff, who tirelessly dug out information, kept pace with the fast-moving news, and assisted me professionally, administratively, and personally.

To my editors and publisher, who added constructive criticism and professionalism to make the book a good read.

To my reviewers, who were supportive and encouraging.

To my agent, who found the right avenue for my book.

PART

1

THE CRISIS

Who are the real insurance crisis culprits? The other guys!
Cartoon by Brad McMillan. Reprinted with permission of Cartoonstock.com.

CHAPTER 1

The Crisis
A Long Time Coming

"We deeply regret that certain of our people failed to live up to our history of dedicated client service. . . ."
—Michael G. Cherkasky, President and CEO, Marsh & McLennan Companies, January 31, 2005

Eliot Spitzer and the Letter that Opened the Insurance Industry's Pandora's Box

The letter—addressed to Eliot Spitzer, the attorney general (AG) of New York State, and postmarked March 30, 2004, Westchester, New York—was unusual. The envelope was penned in hand-blocked writing with no return address. When Deputy Attorney General David D. Brown IV opened the envelope, he found a two-page, single-spaced, typewritten letter, signed "Concerned." Brown, the head of the attorney general's Investment Protection Bureau, studied the contents of the letter carefully.

The writer indicated that there was massive collusion in the insurance industry, and worse, claimed there was bid rigging among insurance brokers and insurance companies. Specifically, the writer accused Marsh & McLennan, the world's largest insurance broker, of "receiving major income for directing business to preferred providers."

After reading the letter, Brown was convinced that it was no hoax. The letter's detailed explanation of wrongdoing indicated that the tipster knew a great deal about the insurance industry. Specifically, the writer claimed that Marsh, instead of negotiating to get the best insurance for its clients, appeared to be steering business to whichever insurer paid Marsh the greatest amount of money. In order to implement this scheme, Marsh had to be colluding with others in the industry to orchestrate the bid process. If the writer was correct, millions of dollars could be going into the pockets of Marsh and the participating insurance carriers, and out of the pockets of unsuspecting insurance customers.

The anonymous note was actually the second communication the attorney general's office had received within the space of two months that warned of illegal activity in the insurance industry. The first letter, which was received on February 10, 2004, was from counsel for the Washington Legal Foundation (WLF), alerting the AG to the fact that the WLF believed insurance brokers were steering their clients to favorite insurance carriers, which was a direct illegal conflict of interest.

Reading the second letter, Brown suspected that something was seriously wrong in the insurance industry. Within minutes, he faxed the letter to his boss, New York State Attorney General Eliot Spitzer. The two spoke by phone soon after.[1] Spitzer, who had built his reputation on uncovering and prosecuting fraud in New York's brokerage and mutual fund industry, found it hard to believe that in light of his recent prosecution of wrongdoers in those areas, the same sort of malfeasance had reared its head again, this time in the insurance industry.

Colluding with others to direct business to preferred insurance providers is bid rigging, which is a crime. Incentives given by an insurer to a broker are a form of contingent commission, which—if not revealed and agreed to by the client—is a kickback. This is also a crime and could be prosecuted under the consumer fraud statutes in New York.

No one had ever launched a full-scale probe of the powerful insurance industry before. Now, that was exactly what Spitzer's team decided to do. Spitzer, 45, was then in his second term as attorney general. The son of an Austrian immigrant and self-made real estate magnate, Spitzer had attended the best schools (Horace Mann, Princeton, and Harvard Law) and grew up around the highest paid corporate executives. After a brief stint as a lawyer in a prestigious Manhattan law firm, he took a job in the attorney general's office.

He returned to private practice, then decided to run for the job of attorney general.

After an unsuccessful try in 1994, Spitzer won the election in his second attempt, in 1998. The young attorney general no doubt was able to draw from things he had learned in his private life regarding the ways in which some elite and successful businesspeople quietly conduct their business. Spitzer and his staff were also mindful of the recent exposure of corporate corruption in such high-profile cases as Enron, Tyco, Adelphia, and WorldCom as well as his own investigation of Wall Street brokers' misrepresentation (the same analyst touting a stock publicly, while deriding it privately) and mutual fund fraud.[2]

Now, it was the insurance industry's turn in the prosecutor's spotlight. Without any special expertise in insurance business law, in the spring and summer of 2004, Spitzer and his staff began intensive research into insurance industry. The AG's office coordinated its efforts with the New York Department of Insurance.

Little known and little used statutes, such as the Martin Act of 1921,[3] allowed the AG's office to assert rights on behalf of the public to inquire into any suspected fraudulent practices, criminal and civil, of any companies engaging in the sale of securities to the public. Spitzer believed he could use this weapon effectively to capture internal memos and e-mails in the insurance industry investigation.[4]

Broad-based subpoenas were issued to well-known names in the insurance industry. Among the brokers subpoenaed were AON Corp., Arthur J. Gallagher & Co., Marsh & McLennan, and the Willis Group; insurers included ACE, American International Group (AIG), Aetna, CIGNA, General Re, Hartford Financial, ING, MetLife, Munich Re, and UnumProvident.

Spitzer's office's intense investigation hit pay dirt. Reviewing numerous internal memos, e-mails, and other documents received as a result of the subpoenas, a law student interning in the AG's office found the smoking gun: an e-mail soliciting a sham bid from an insurance company in order to help Marsh steer business to the insurance company it favored in this transaction (the one paying the highest fee). It was clear and unmistakable direct evidence of Marsh's criminal bid rigging. For example, Spitzer's office obtained an e-mail sent from a Marsh broker to an underwriter at Zurich Financial Services:

> . . . seeking a phony bid for an insurance contract that was being steered to one of Zurich's competitors, AIG: "Can you give me a protective indication on this. It is an AIG renewal and AIG already quoted it so just give me a bad price with higher per occ. [occurence], and attachment, and then we can be done with this."[5]

Bid rigging is a well-orchestrated collusive maneuver that requires that several players be in on the scam. The principal broker hired by the client knows in advance the rate and terms of his or her preferred insurer (usually the one that pays the principal broker the highest fee or commission). The principal broker goes through the motions of getting a "competitive bid," but actually asks another broker or insurer, who is in on the scam, to supply a B-Quote or B-bid. That bidder is told the premium and terms of the preferred insurer's bid and obligingly submits a B-Quote. The B-Quote or B-bid is named for the second letter in the alphabet or shorthand for the second best bid and is either at a higher rate or with more onerous terms than the first bid. This naturally steers the client to the principal broker's preferred insurer. The principal broker gets a high commission, the winning insurance company writes the policy and gets the higher than market premium, the broker or insurer supplying the B-Quote is promised future business, and the unsuspecting client pays a higher premium or gets lesser coverage (or both).

By late summer 2004, Spitzer's office concluded that the anonymous tip was accurate. There appeared to be significant evidence of large-scale civil and criminal wrongdoing[6] in the insurance industry.

Spitzer Files His Complaint

On October 14, 2004, the New York attorney general, joined by the New York State Department of Insurance, rocked the insurance world when he filed a complaint in the New York State Supreme Court, *New York State v. Marsh & McLennan Cos.* The complaint, with nearly 100 pages of exhibits, also referred to several major insurers or insurance service companies—American International Group (AIG), ACE Ltd., Hartford Financial Services, Munich American Risk Partners—alleging conflict of interest and bid rigging. It included charges of fraudulent business practices, violations of antitrust law, securities fraud, unjust enrichment, and common-law fraud.

On the same day, as if to emphasize the gravity of the industry problems, Spitzer announced that two insurance executives of AIG, the largest insurance carrier in the world, had pleaded guilty in criminal court to "scheme to defraud," a felony under the criminal laws of the state of New York. Spitzer's team was proceeding on two fronts, civil liability and criminal liability for corporations and individuals. The lines between civil and criminal liability may have been somewhat blurred, but the charges were extremely effective.[6]

Spitzer's complaint alleged that the windfall to Marsh & McLennan created by this scheme was a kickback, and that the brokers or insurers who knowingly supplied B-Quotes were criminally liable. For example, the complaint alleged the following:

> The enormous size of these profits [to Marsh] is not happenstance, but the result of careful planning. Marsh reconfigured its brokerage business, centralizing power in a group based in Manhattan. Marsh created lists of those insurance companies whose products its employees were to sell more vigorously to clients, lists based not on price or service, but on the amount of money the insurance companies would pay Marsh. It rewarded those employees who sold clients more insurance from these complicit insurance companies, and it chastised those who did not.[7]

Elsewhere, the complaint cited an e-mail from a Marsh employee to CNA Insurance:

> "'[P]er my voicemail, we need to show a CNA proposal. I will outline below the leading programs (ACE & Zurich). I want to present a CNA program that is reasonably competitive, but will not be a winner.' [The Marsh employee] proceeded to reveal the ACE and Zurich quotes on the project and then proposed numbers that CNA should quote in order to lose the bid but still appear to have been competitive. Although CNA never authorized Marsh to submit this bid, it was submitted to [the insurance client] as a legitimate competing bid."[8]

According to Spitzer's office, the bid rigging fraudulently inflated the cost to business customers by millions of dollars (the AG said it represented more than 30 percent of Marsh's annual revenues), resulting in illegal profits for brokers and insurers and a major misrepresentation of their income.

At the end of January 2005, just three months after the Spitzer complaint was filed, Marsh & McLennan agreed to pay to the state of New York restitution and fines totaling $850 million to settle the bid rigging and other charges against the company. In addition to regulatory fines, Spitzer announced that as the funds, which were to be paid in increments, were received, all of the money would be returned to the victims of these insurance practices. (This has since been done.)

By August 2005, less than one year after Spitzer's complaint was filed, Marsh's stock price had fallen by 40 percent.[9]

The Prosecutorial Net Snares AIG and Some Key Players

Spitzer's group dragged old-line brokerage and insurance companies as well as key executives into its prosecutorial net. Among those focused on was one previously well-respected industry leader and innovator, AIG's CEO Maurice R. "Hank" Greenberg. Spitzer charged Greenberg with making sham deals and using deceptive accounting practices in an attempt to increase the value of AIG's stock. Spitzer claimed he had evidence to show that Greenberg, with assistance from employees of a major reinsurance company (Warren Buffett's Gen Re), colluded to place on AIG's books a $500 million sham transaction that created the appearance that AIG had an additional $500 million in reserves with which to pay claims. The effect of this bogus entry, Spitzer asserted, created a totally misleading picture of the company's financial strength, putting the public, shareholders, and policyholders in jeopardy. The result of the Spitzer charges against AIG and its executives was devastating.

To shareholders, policyholders, and regulators, these actions would appear to be fraud. Even in a company as large as AIG (with $116 billion in annual revenue),[10] they distorted the true financial picture of the company and created the false impression that there was significantly more money on the company's balance sheet than there actually was—which, in turn, misrepresented the true value of the company's stock. The appearance of sham transactions was a very serious matter to AIG's board of directors.

As a result, shortly after the Spitzer charges, the AIG board of directors put enormous pressure on Hank Greenberg, a leader in the industry who had built AIG into a powerhouse since he joined the company in the early 1960s. On March 15, 2005, at the age of seventy-nine, Greenberg unceremoniously resigned as AIG's CEO and chairman of the board.

Soon after, on March 31, 2005, AIG's new leaders admitted to multimillion-dollar accounting irregularities and stated that several transactions "appear to have been structured for the sole purpose or primary purpose of accomplishing a desired accounting effect." AIG revealed that the impact of the accounting errors would lower its book value by $1.7 billion.[11] In the end, the Securities and Exchange Commission forced AIG to restate its profits downward for the previous five years. The revisions eliminated approximately $2 billion of shareholder equity and approximately $4 billion of profits.

In addition, AIG paid $1.64 billion to settle allegations that the company used deceptive accounting practices to mislead regulatory agencies and investors. This settlement, believed to be the largest deal ever concluded by regulators with a single company, also required the company to change its business practices to ensure that there were proper accounting procedures in place in the future.[12]

The decline in AIG's prestige as a leader in the insurance industry had a direct impact on its stock value. For example, from mid-February 2005, when the government probes were announced, to March 31, 2005, AIG stock went down precipitously by 22 percent.[13] By March 2006, AIG reported its fourth-quarter earnings had sunk by 72 percent, hurt by the huge legal settlement charges and hurricane-related losses.[14] All of the criminal charges against Hank Greenberg ultimately were dropped by AIG's office because of lack of direct evidence,[15] but the impact of other AIG executives' guilty pleas and the admission by AIG of civil accounting deception still resonates.

The Widening Storm

The Spitzer investigation of the insurance industry revealed wrongdoing at the highest levels. Starting with the world's largest broker (Marsh) and continuing with allegations against a top executive of one of the world's largest insurance companies (Greenberg of AIG), it reverberated around the country and around the world.

Spitzer's actions were not without detractors. He was criticized by some as ruthless or as pursuing the high-profile investigation purely for political gain. Shortly after Spitzer and his team announced the filing of criminal and civil charges against members of the insurance industry in October 2004, Tom Donohue, president of the U.S. Chamber of Commerce, issued a statement on behalf of the Chamber charging that Spitzer was acting as the "judge, jury and executioner" in these investigations. Spitzer defended his actions and those of his staff and replied forcefully on national television:

> Tom Donohue cannot show you one fact we've alleged that is wrong. . . . [H]e is, I think, tarnishing the reputations of many of his members who don't want that sort of voice out there saying that illegal conduct is good. It isn't. My job has been to reveal facts, to bring the cases. And I think if you ask any investor, if you ask any executive, do you want to live in a world where analytical work is fraudulent, where mutual funds are diluting and skimming profits, where insurance companies are bid rigging, I think they will tell you no. The reason is that those behavior patterns cut against the market as we want it to operate.[16]

On November 16, 2004, just a few weeks after Spitzer filed the complaint against Marsh in New York, the U.S. Senate Governmental Affairs Subcommittee on Financial Management, the Budget, and International Security convened hearings to look into industry improprieties, including potential conflicts of interest in the insurance brokerage business and the adequacy of the current insurance regulatory framework. Spitzer, California's Insurance Commissioner John Garamendi, and Connecticut's Attorney General Richard Blumenthal were among those who testified.

At the hearing, Spitzer detailed the bid rigging and fraud charges he had brought against the industry and discussed the deleterious effects these practices were having on the economy. Garamendi, who was widely interviewed on television after his testimony, accused many in the insurance industry of "above all else, flat-out greed." Garamendi (now California's lieutenant governor)—a charismatic presence in government for more than thirty years—has been an outspoken critic of the insurance industry and a champion of consumers' insurance interests.

In his Senate testimony, Garamendi stated:

> . . . [I]nsurance brokers have routinely violated the trust of the clients they represent by entering into agreements—whether they are called PSAs (Preferred Service Agreements), MSAs (Master Service Agreements), contingent commission agreements or the like—which secretly paid them hundreds of millions of dollars in additional compensation from the insurance companies that they recommended to their clients and which sold insurance to their clients. In addition, insurers secretly provided brokers and agents with lavish trips and other incentives based on the amount of business the broker placed with them.[17]

At the conclusion of the congressional hearings, Garamendi promised to investigate any insurance companies operating in California that were part of the scheme. For the next three years, the California Department of Insurance proceeded aggressively and successfully against the violators.

Richard Blumenthal, the Connecticut attorney general who has also been in the forefront of the fight for insurance reform, advised Congress that his investigations had uncovered evidence of illegal and improper anticonsumer activities "ranging from bid rigging to fraudulent, concealed commissions and secret payoffs, to flagrant conflicts of interest—all stifling competition and inflating insurance costs to consumers." Blumenthal commended Spitzer for his "historic leadership" and added that "the scale and magnitude of corrupt practices [in the insurance industry] continue to mount and much more remains to be done." Blumenthal promised that his state prosecutors would pursue cases aggressively, and did so over the next several years.[18]

Other Probes

And there were other probes. On January 7, 2005, the New York State Assembly Standing Committee on Insurance convened its own hearing into the problems in the industry. Key witnesses were Attorney General Spitzer and New York Superintendent of Insurance Gregory V. Serio. Spitzer accused many brokers and insurance companies of engaging in "systematic fraud and market manipulation," adding that the evidence of fraud was on a scale far larger than he had anticipated at the start of his investigation. Spitzer also said that the practices were widespread and affected all types of insurance, including personal (such as homeowners and auto) insurance as well as commercial (business) insurance, and extended to the reinsurance market.[19]

During the hearings, it was disclosed that New York Insurance Department regulators were aware of the bid-rigging practices and had actually published guidelines in 1998[20] to eliminate bid rigging and to require disclosure of broker compensation. However, the Insurance Department had done nothing to enforce or follow up on compliance. Instead, in the intervening years, the fraud appeared to grow unchecked. Why there had been no regulatory follow-up was never adequately explained. Serio defended the department's lack of performance, but admitted that insurance regulatory reform was needed.[21]

What is so shocking about the bid-rigging investigation is that many in the industry knew, even before the announcement of the charges, that these practices had been common for years and were part of a much larger pattern. The fact that the New York regulators, usually known to be strong watchdogs, had published guidelines to avoid this practice but did nothing to identify the violators and root out the problem is an egregious example of the holes in the regulatory net under the current insurance system.

The probe grew even larger. In May 2005, the Federal Bureau of Investigation (FBI) announced that it would be looking into possible criminal activity[22] in the insurance industry, stating that it did not want to be caught napping if the next big financial crisis was insurance-related corporate fraud.[23] The Bureau feared a repeat of the savings and loan industry crisis in the 1980s, when more than one thousand Savings and Loan (S&L) institutions failed, resulting in a $190 billion bailout by the FSLIC, and the corporate fraud allegations against Enron, Tyco, Adelphia, WorldCom, and others in 2001 and 2002.

While the FBI's announcement highlighted the serious nature of the allegations against the insurance industry, many observers believed that the federal inquiries by the FBI began very late in the game—almost one full year after Spitzer's state probe started. It was a glaring reminder of the current lack of federal authority and the inadequacy of federal enforcement in this area.

Settlements and Convictions

The accusations by New York Attorney General Spitzer, California Insurance Commissioner Garamendi, and Connecticut Attorney General Blumenthal quickly began to gather momentum. The number of companies involved in the investigation expanded, and by early 2005, most insurance companies and executives were cooperating. As a result, substantial settlements were negotiated with many of the companies for violations they had committed. Insurance and brokerage companies offered millions of dollars in cash settlements in an attempt to get the scandal behind them and avoid deeper inquiries.

The settlements came rapidly and reached dizzying proportions. In addition to reaching settlement with Marsh & McLennan for a huge $850 million refund and reform agreements, New York entered into similar multimillion-dollar agreements with other insurance companies. On March 4, 2005, AON, the world's second largest insurance brokerage company, agreed to pay $190 million and to adopt reforms to eliminate incentive fees paid to brokers. Willis, another large national broker, settled with Spitzer's office for $50 million. Broker Arthur J. Gallagher & Co. settled for $35 million.

As the New York State civil investigation continued through 2005, so did the criminal charges. Some insurers and brokers admitted their criminal complicity. Others did not. Some executives pleaded the U.S. Constitution's Fifth Amendment privilege against self-incrimination. By mid-2005, fifteen insurance executives had pleaded guilty to a variety of insurance fraud charges, including scheme to defraud in the first degree (a class E felony carrying a maximum sentence of 1 to 4 years in prison) and scheme to defraud in the second degree (a Class A misdemeanor with a maximum sentence of 1 year in jail). Those pleading guilty included insurance executives at Marsh, Zurich American Insurance Co., ACE, and AIG. As of March 27, 2006, the New York AG's office reported that twenty insurance company executives and officers had pleaded guilty to criminal offenses.[24] As of November 2007, those pleading guilty were still awaiting sentencing. The New York AG's office had recovered more than $2.6 billion for the victimized customers from the insurance brokers and insurance companies involved.[25] Connecticut's record was also impressive. On August 31, 2005, the Connecticut AG's office announced that it had made a $30 million settlement with Hilb Rogal & Hobbs (HRH), the nation's eighth largest insurance agency, for steering clients to certain insurers in exchange for hidden commissions. In addition, on April 26, 2006, Blumenthal announced that ACE had agreed to pay $80 million to settle bid-rigging allegations.

Between 2005 and 2007, California Commissioner Garamendi's team was able to effectuate settlements with a number of companies: Zurich American Insurance Co., requiring full disclosure of commissions and a $172 million financial settlement to be shared by California policyholders; Marsh & McLennan, establishing the broker's legal obligation to disclose commissions and Marsh's agreement to do so; MetLife, CIGNA, Prudential, The Hartford, and UnumProvident, requiring them to disclose to prospective insureds any commissions paid to brokers; and Universal Life Resources (a large employee benefits firm), establishing the broker's fiduciary duty to its clients in the employee benefits area.

Many other states also launched investigations. In 2005, fifteen states (California, Connecticut, Florida, Hawaii, Illinois, Maryland, Massachusetts, New Jersey, New York, Ohio, Oregon, Pennsylvania, Texas, Virginia, and West Virginia) announced that they would implement their own investigations, continue their current investigations, or join a coalition of states conducting investigations.

Multistate Settlements

On March 27, 2006, Connecticut's attorney general's office announced that it was part of a $153 million multistate settlement (also involving Illinois and New York) with Zurich American Insurance Co. for its part in the bid-rigging scheme. Zurich also agreed to adopt sweeping business reforms and to repay millions to policyholders and taxpayers for illegal actions that spanned several years. The AG's press release stated that since "at least the mid-1990s," Zurich and other insurance companies had paid hundreds of millions of dollars in "contingent commissions" to the world's largest insurance brokers (including Marsh, AON, Willis, and Gallagher), "as well as thousands of smaller brokers and independent agents."

Connecticut Department of Consumer Protection Commissioner Edwin R. Rodriguez said, "Zurich's business model was based on prearranged dishonesty. It provided them with an unfair competitive advantage by directing a scheme of paying undisclosed fees to brokers who funneled them business. This deceptive practice cost policyholders millions of dollars in premiums that trickled down to consumers in higher insurance costs."

Illinois Attorney General Lisa Madigan, also involved in the settlement, said:

Our investigation revealed that Zurich schemed with insurance brokers and other insurers to rig bids, behavior that led policyholders to pay more for insurance. Zurich also secretly paid contingent commissions to brokers in exchange for the brokers steering business to Zurich. This settlement, along with other recent similar settlements, will go a long way toward ensuring transparency and fairness in this industry.

On December 21, 2006, the Connecticut AG's office announced that the Chubb Group had agreed to pay $17 million to a Connecticut, Illinois, and New York settlement fund, including payment of a fine, restitution to customers, and hundreds of thousands of dollars in investigation fees incurred by the states. Chubb also agreed to adopt landmark business reforms, including the elimination of contingent commissions. On July 27, 2007, the Connecticut AG's office also announced that the same three states were part of a $115 million settlement with The Hartford. The office's press release on the settlement included this surprising piece of information regarding the insurer's deceptive sales practices:

"The Hartford agreements with brokers Acordia and HRH (Hilb Rogal & Hobbs) were particularly successful in steering personal lines customers to Hartford. Both agreements called for wholesale "book rolling," or switching of consumers to The Hartford without any disclosure of the brokers' financial motivation for making the switch. Many consumers also believed their policies were being serviced by HRH or Acordia. In reality, customers were asked to call a service center owned and staffed by The Hartford. When HRH customers called The Hartford service center, The Hartford answered the phone as if it were HRH. When Acordia customers called The Hartford service center, The Hartford did not tell the customers they were speaking to their insurer, not their supposedly independent insurance agent."

On August 4, 2007, Blumenthal's office announced that the St. Paul Travelers Companies had agreed to stop paying contingent commissions on certain types of insurance, and that Connecticut would receive part of a $40 million multistate (again, with Illinois and New York) penalty payment in settlement of bid-rigging charges. In addition, the company agreed to pay $37 million in restitution to the victimized customers. Blumenthal called the St. Paul Travelers settlement "another blow to a business culture of kickbacks."

Many state investigations were ongoing at the time of this writing, with many additional millions being repaid to customers along with the promise of reform.

■ ■ ■

The effort put into dealing with insurance fraud yielded positive results. However, the problem with state prosecution is that, while laudable, it was piecemeal. Different states have different laws with regard to civil and criminal liability in insurance cases, and some states remain unable or unwilling to implement a full-court-press strategy. State prosecution was also reactive, taking action after the fact, rather than proactive—preventing the improper activity from happening in the first place, and doing it uniformly in all states.

In fairness to the states, criticism of insurance industry regulation has not been directed solely at the states. Eliot Spitzer, in a featured address before an association of business writers in 2005, pointed a finger directly at Washington and the attitude of the administration of President George W. Bush, which he said fostered the culture that led to the behavior of the insurance industry. Spitzer bemoaned the fact that although the insurance industry had thus far paid more than $1 billion in restitution in settlement of its misdeeds, "not a word has come out of the White House about maybe there being a structural problem in the insurance industry."[26] Spitzer's opinion was that there was a fundamental defect in the way the insurance industry was regulated.

The Current Crisis

The long overdue investigation of the insurance industry received so much attention because it hit a nerve. It raised a topic that no one really wanted to focus on publicly before—the erosion of trust in the insurance industry, one of the nation's oldest and most venerable institutions. Insurance customers had always relied on the fact that at some point in the future, their insurance company would be there to pay them, fairly and promptly, for their legitimate claims. Now, business and individual consumers are not so confident in the insurance industry. Unless there are significant changes in attitude and oversight, consumer confidence will not be restored. Before that confidence can be restored, many ominous matters and trends will have to be dealt with, including insolvency, embezzlement, international takeovers, unpaid claims, and lack of uniform laws.

The continuing criticism emanating from respected agencies and organizations, such as the U.S. GAO (Government Accountability Office) and the CFA (Consumer Federation of America), as well as troubling statistics published annually by the controlling industry association, the NAIC (National Association of Insurance Commissioners), demonstrate that these problems are still unresolved. In the next decade, even more issues will emerge.

Many consumers and observers who have been following these developments over the years (including this writer) now fear that their insurance company may not be able to deliver its part of the bargain: the peace of mind and trust for which we all pay dearly. They are concerned that if the insurance system continues to function as it does today, the companies may not be there in the future to pay their claims, and the peace of mind they have paid for may become their worst nightmare.

Insurance, one of the country's biggest industries—with more than $1.4 trillion in annual premiums earned per year—is in a crisis, and is on the brink of major exposure and massive change.[27]

Insurance is an important part of our economy and society. Each year in the United States, people collectively pay a staggering sum to insurance companies. Insurance is in the top four expenditures of the average consumer (housing, transportation, food, and insurance), according to the U.S. Bureau of Labor Statistics.[28] Insurance affects us all, and unresolved problems in the industry can have a significant financial and emotional impact on the average insured person. According to the BLS, the average household spends 6.8 percent of their budget for insurance annually,[29] or $3,400 for a family earning an income of $50,000 annually. In some cases, families can spend more than 10 percent of their budget on insurance. That is a significant amount of money for anyone. Some businesses spend even more than 10 percent.

In the United States, 257 million people have insurance in one form or another (health, home, life, auto, business insurance, and others), and virtually everyone is affected by insurance regulations. Even the 47 million citizens in the United States who sadly cannot afford or cannot get health insurance are affected by insurance principles (or lack thereof) created by the government.[30]

Most consumers are not acquainted with the industry's problems and are surprised to find there is no federal oversight of the insurance industry. Many also are unaware that their insurance company may not be able to pay their claims and that state officials may not be able to protect them.

Most state regulators have been struggling with the growing problems and trends over the years, but are either unable or unwilling to exercise proper oversight. State regulators are supposed to act as watchdogs for the consumer and oversee the smooth flow of the insurers' rates and forms, market conduct, claims handling, and administrative needs. In the main, the state regulators have lost their ability to be a safety net for the consumer. They have not been able to increase efficiencies or lower costs for the insurer. In fact, many state regulators, facing budgetary constraints, are treading water in a sea of increasingly national and international issues, desperately trying to keep themselves from sinking. State regulators and staff dutifully attend NAIC quarterly meetings, afraid to admit publicly that the insurance system is in trouble; if they do admit it, they have not been effective in getting all the states to act together to make the fundamental changes needed. (More will be said about state regulation in subsequent chapters.)

Former regulators admit that the state system of insurance regulation is untenable. Some insurer associations now realize that the time for transformation is now. Even insurance executives currently working in the industry predict that the problems presented are so large that they will result in massive changes.[31] Politicians are taking these problems seriously.

Until there is uniformity and fairness in the creation, delivery, operation, marketing, sales, claims handling, review, accountability, and enforcement of insurance industry law in the United States, these issues will not be resolved.

The "Vulture Culture"

The problems of the insurance industry affect everyone who is insured and even some who are not. They emanate from what I call a *vulture culture*—that is, a poorly regulated, uncontrolled business climate, where negative forces are allowed to flourish and prey on the unwary.

As you read this book, you will find a list of difficulties facing the insurance industry. Your first tendency might be to dismiss each of the problems cited as isolated or unrelated incidents, happening to this individual company, that executive, this claimant, that regulator, this state, or that region. But as you step back from each of the close-ups and look at the insurance industry as a whole, you will find that these incidents are not isolated or unrelated. They are happening in every corner of the country, to many, many companies, executives, claimants, regulators, states, and regions. They all are part of a larger culture, and the problems are having a huge impact on the public.

In a sense, the military strategy of "divide and conquer" has been employed effectively in the insurance industry. The McCarran-Ferguson Act of 1945 is the insurance industry's controlling law, passed by Congress when insurance was essentially local and not the international business it is today. McCarran-Ferguson, in addition to exempting the insurance industry from anti-trust laws, mandates that each state, not the federal government, regulate the "business of insurance" within its respective borders. As a result, the insurance industry is the only major industry in the United States affecting our lives on a daily basis with virtually no federal oversight. Each state, independent of the other states, regulates insurance within its borders; and the state regulators are coordinated by the NAIC—an entity with no statutory mandate, no power of enforcement, and no statutory duty to bring problems to the public's attention.

Without our noticing it, this vulture culture has grown up around us. This culture has led to a crisis in the insurance industry, which, in turn, has led to finger pointing from government, lawyers, healthcare providers, businesses, insurance companies, and consumers about just who is the real culprit. Rather than working together to find a solution, each sector blames the other. If this vulture culture is allowed to thrive, hundreds of thousands of unwary consumers will continue to be hurt, and additional millions of dollars will be needlessly lost by both insurers and consumers.

This crisis, long in coming, was predictable and, even more unfortunate, avoidable. Not all those involved in and around the insurance community are contributing to it—a large majority of them are not—but because the unresolved issues are pervasive, the insurance system is in serious disrepair and only a major systemic change will fix it.

Eliot Spitzer and his team's allegations, and the other investigations that followed, focused worldwide attention on several problem areas—bid rigging, steering clients, collusion, and deceptive accounting—shockingly carried out by trusted top-of-the-line insurance brokerage companies, insurers, and key executives. The investigations into the previously quiet insurance industry have opened a Pandora's box of ugly problems. As Americans, with a rich history of innovation and fortitude in the face of adversity, we can find a solution. This book offers an answer.

Notes

1. I am grateful to Steve Fishman for his excellent article "Inside Eliot's Army," *New York Magazine,* January 10, 2005 (accessible at nymag.com/nymetro/news/politics/newyork/features10815) for some of the details of the anonymous tip that started Spitzer's investigations into the insurance industry and the facts that set the stage for these investigations. Corroborating the content of the anonymous note was an informative article by Peter Elkind, "Spitzer's Crusade," *Fortune,* November 15, 2004. For further details about the WLF letter, see also Sean M. Fitzpatrick, "The Small Laws: Eliot Spitzer and the Way to Insurance Market Reform," *Fordham Law Review,* May 2006, vol. 74. (Fitzpatrick is a lecturer in law at the University of Connecticut School of Law and senior vice president and special counsel, The Chubb Corporation.)

2. When he was first elected as New York State's attorney general in 1998, few believed that Spitzer would, or could, carry out his many campaign promises, which included establishing "law and order, . . . eliminating white collar crime, . . . restoring confidence in the marketplace, . . . attacking deception and conflicts of interest, . . . rooting out the guilty." In fact, he and his team succeeded in rooting out fraud and corruption in the securities brokerage and mutual fund industries, as well as in many other business sectors, including the insurance industry. Spitzer became governor of New York in January 2007.

3. The Martin Act of 1921, New York State Consolidated Laws, General Business Law, Chapter 20, Article 23-A, Section 352 et seq., "Fraudulent practices in respect to stocks, bonds and other securities." The act gives the attorney general extraordinary powers of subpoena and investigation when criminal and civil fraudulent securities practices are suspected.

4. Eric Dinallo, working in Spitzer's office, was credited with dusting off the Martin Act and showing how it could be effectively used to investigate the

insurance industry. In 2007, under Governor Spitzer, Dinallo became superintendent of the New York State Insurance Department. Dinallo's credentials
are impressive; in addition to serving in the AG's office, he had been an executive with insurance broker Willis as well as a prosecutor.

5. Fitzpatrick, "The Small Laws"; see also Kate Kelley, "In Spitzer's Office, Hours
of Drudgery, Moments of 'Gotcha!' " *Wall Street Journal*, October 27, 2004.
Also, see press release from New York Attorney General's Office, March 27,
2006, quoting the Marsh email to Zurich Financial Services.

6. Spitzer's actions illustrate an important principle: A corporation may be criminally liable for the illegal acts of its directors, employees, and agents. His
actions are also an example of a new prosecutorial weapon, the blurring of
lines between civil and criminal liability. This means that some corporate
practices, which traditionally were considered wrongs against individuals or
violations of contract law, are now viewed as crimes against society, and actions pursued in the past under criminal law may now be brought in the civil
court system as well. Prosecutors fearing they cannot meet the stricter burden
of proof in a criminal case (beyond a reasonable doubt) now have the flexibility to bring a civil action where the burden of proof (a fair preponderance of
the evidence) is easier to meet. The combination of criminal and civil actions
has resulted in massive monetary settlements and reform from corporations
as well as many executive convictions. This approach by states is laudable, but
it is piecemeal since different states have different laws (both civil and criminal), and some states are unable or unwilling to implement the full-press
strategy.

7. Complaint, *State v. Marsh & McLennan* Cos., No. 04403342 (N.Y. Sup. Ct.
Oct. 14, 2004), available at http://www.oag.state.ny.us/press/2004/oct/oct14a_
04_attach1.pdf. See paragraph 30 of the Marsh & McLennan Companies complaint, and paragraph 72 of the AG complaint.

8. Ibid., paragraph 32.

9. AFX News Limited, AFX International Focus, August 4, 2005.

10. 2006 AIG Annual report.

11. Jenny Anderson, "Insurer Admits Bad Accounting in Several Deals," *New
York Times*, March 31, 2005, available at http://www.nytimes.com/2005/03/
31/business/31insure.html?_r = 1&oref = slogin&pagewanted = all&
position = . The *Times* article also quoted a March 30, 2005, report by William
Wilt, an analyst with Morgan Stanley: "The depth and breadth of troubles
and apparent lack of accounting controls at AIG is alarming." See also Tom
Kirkendall, "Absolutely Enronesque," *Houston's Clear Thinkers*, March 31,
2005.

12. Jenny Anderson, "Senior AIG Executive Is Said to Be Ready to Cooperate in Inquiry on Accounting Methods," *New York Times*, May 14, 2005; see also Anderson, "AIG Profit Is Reduced by $4 Billion," *New York Times*, June 1, 2005, and Associated Press, "Two Charges against AIG's Greenberg Dropped; Spitzer aide says four left concerning deception are 'heart of the case,' available at http://www.msnbc.msn.com/id/14704060/.

13. NYSE records. See also Kirkendall, "Absolutely Enronesque." *Houston's Clear Thinkers,* March 31, 2005, available at http://blog.kir.com/archives/2005/03/absolutely_enro.asp.

14. "AIG Earnings drop 72 percent in fourth quarter," Reuters, March 16, 2006.

15. Ian McDonald and Leslie Scism, "AIG's Ex Clears A Hurdle But Faces More," *Wall Street Journal*, Friday, November 25, 2005, available at http://online.wsj.com/article/SB113288840104206370.html?mod=home_whats_news_us.

16. Neil Cavuto interview with Eliot Spitzer, *Your World with Neil Cavuto*, Fox News Network, February 17, 2005.

17. Commissioner Garamendi's comment "above all else, flat-out greed" was carried on most national television networks, shortly after his testimony, on November 16, 2004. The actual testimony was presented earlier in the day to the Subcommittee on Financial Management, the Budget, and International Security Committee on Governmental Affairs, US Senate http://www.insurance.ca.gov/0250-insurers/0500-legal-info/0500-gen-legal-info/0700-broker-compensation/upload/BrokerCommissionsTestimonyUSSenate11-16-04.pdf.

18. "Oversight Hearing on Insurance Brokerage Practices, including Potential Conflicts of Interest and the Adequacy of the Current Regulatory Framework," November 16, 2004, Washington, D.C. See also InsuranceJournal.com, November 16, 2004, and numerous other news sources.

19. "New York Attorney General and Superintendent of Insurance Testify Before Assembly Insurance Committee re: Insurance Broker Compensation Practices," InsuranceLaw@manatt, January 13, 2005.

20. New York Insurance Department Circular Letter Number 22, 1998, prepared under the direction of then Insurance Superintendent Neil D. Levin.

21. One theory for the inaction was that just as Superintendent Levin was ready to implement the anti–bid-rigging circular, he became CEO of the New York–New Jersey Port Authority, and that the new superintendent, Gregory V. Serio, believed the circular guidelines went beyond New York law. Serio, in his 2005 testimony before the New York State Legislature, defended his department's failure to enforce, stating that there was no direct prohibition against contingent commissions in the New York Insurance Law (although there was a direct prohibition against consumer fraud). He further stated that the department

had not received complaints about broker compensation from purchasers of insurance (although at the time customers could not have known about the improper compensation).

22. "Criminal activity" is any activity that violates state or federal statutes, ordinances, or codes. "Illegal acts" is a broader term that refers to violations of laws and governmental regulations, whether criminal or civil.

23. "FBI Targets Insurers in Widening Fraud Probe; Industry Responds," Insurance Journal May 5, 2005, available at http://www.insurancejournal.com/news/national/2005/05/05/54728.htm.

24. "Three More Guilty Pleas in Insurance Scandal," consumeraffairs.com, February 15, 2005.

25. New York State Attorney General's Office, press release, March 27, 2006.

26. Eliot Spitzer, 2005 address to the Society of American Business Editors and Writers, Seattle, Washington.

27. National Association of Insurance Commissioners, Insurance Department Resources Report, 2006, published 2007.

28. United States Bureau of Labor Statistics.

29. Ibid.

30. U.S. Department of Commerce, Economics and Statistics Administration, (2002).

31. Statement by Stephen Sills, October 23, 2004. Sills is the founder, president, and CEO of Darwin Professional Underwriters. He founded and was the CEO of Executive Risk, specialists in director and officer liability insurance, which he sold to Chubb in 1999.

"It covers you for everything except fire, accident, illness, loss, personal injury, or death."
Cartoon by Neil Bennett. Reprinted with permission of Cartoonstock.com.

CHAPTER 2

How the Industry Got Where It Is
A Rogues' Gallery

"In Chattanooga, and particularly inside the offices of one of the city's largest employers, UnumProvident, the name of former company CEO J. Harold Chandler is mud."

—Drew Ruble, Editor, *Business TN Magazine,* Nashville, Tennessee, July 2006

Executive Accountability
J. Harold Chandler, CEO, UnumProvident

Who would have thought that an old-line, reputable insurance carrier, Provident Life and Accident, would hire J. Harold Chandler as its chief executive? Yet in 1993, faced with a run of unanticipated claims and significant losses, the Provident board turned to Chandler, an industry outsider. A banker who specialized in turning around bad loans, Chandler, age 43, had no operational executive experience in the insurance industry. A former college football quarterback with a winning Southern can-do style, he quickly set out to implement his strategy.

According to facts alleged in thousands of lawsuits against the company (as well as in several class action suits) and elsewhere, that strategy resulted in a series of tactics aimed at rejecting policyholders' legitimate claims. The trials resulted in millions of dollars in judgments against Provident.[1]

Problems with Provident's Own-Occ Policies

For decades, Provident Life and Accident Insurance Company, headquartered in Chattanooga, Tennessee, was headed by the conservative, philanthropic McClellan family. In the 1980s, Provident created an attractive disability policy targeted to high-income, highly motivated professionals such as doctors and lawyers. The "Own-Occ" policy, as it is known, offered significant monthly benefits if the insured person became disabled and unable to carry out the specific duties of his or her practice or specialty. (Many policies paid a professional between $5,000 and $15,000 a month, sometimes as much as 70 percent of his/her income, depending on the premium.) For example, a physician who became disabled, could not perform his or her surgical specialty, and instead began to teach medicine could receive a teaching salary and still be eligible to receive monthly Own-Occ benefits from the insurance company.

In the late 1980s, sales of the Provident Own-Occ policy exceeded expectations. The plan, which offered low premiums and good monthly benefits, represented a major part of Provident's income. As a result, Provident's bottom line was looking good, and profitability increased each year. Provident and other insurers believed the professional income group they were targeting had minimum risk; that is, it was the category of individuals least likely to file a disability benefits claim. However, in the early 1990s, the number of claims increased significantly. As this group of professionals aged, there was an unpredicted increase in diseases and stress-related illnesses, and Provident had not put aside an amount of money, or "reserves," sufficient to meet all of these claims. Sales of individual disability insurance in the early 1990s made up a significant portion of the annual income for Provident (30 percent), but the claims from individual disability during that period threatened to swamp the company, wiping out the profits.

By 1993, the Provident board of directors had become alarmed. In that year, for the first time, the company showed an annual loss—$93 million.[2] The pressure increased when auditors forced Provident to beef up reserves by an additional $483 million in order to pay off future claims.

With losses mounting, the Provident board of directors decided it had to do something drastic. Toward the end of 1993, they hired J. Harold Chandler. Chandler's overall strategy for recovery was simple and effective: Provident would continue to collect the premiums on existing policies but would stop selling new Own-Occ policies. In addition, the claims department, in an aggressive change in Provident's corporate culture, was directed to "scrub the files," which meant an in-depth review to find any reason to terminate claims. Delay and denial of claim payments became commonplace and a major part of the turnaround plan. Chandler declared a sense of urgency to all his employees and brought a doomsday mind-set to the company. Employees heard his message: Provident had to be profitable at any cost.

The Strategy: The Quarterly Scrub and Other Tactics

From public records and with twenty-twenty hindsight, a clear picture emerges of how Chandler's plan worked to reduce claims, cut the company's losses, and create a profit.

Chandler created weekly "roundtable" meetings of key executives and medical personnel to discuss and eliminate key claims— those that paid out more than $5,000 per month.[3] One executive meeting agenda targeted the "elimination of the bad block of business" (in other words, the Own-Occ individual disability block of business).

The CEO also implemented the "quarterly scrub," where high-cost claim files were scrutinized by top claims personnel looking for mistakes in the claimants' application or other file anomalies.[4] This tactic, which some industry observers call unethical, is known as post-claim underwriting, and often includes not only a review of the statements on the claimant's initial application for insurance but also a review of past medical records to find any discrepancy that might allow the company to terminate the claim. Stronger investigative techniques (such as criminal background checks, surveillance, forensic financial audits) were also used on certain targeted high payout claimants in an effort to find any inconsistency.

Another technique employed by Provident to terminate claims was through independent medical examinations (IMEs). The term "independent," however, was a misnomer. Under the terms of the disability policy, the claimant was required to submit to an examination by a medical consultant chosen and paid by Provident. In general, the lawsuits claimed that doctors filing medical reports favorable to the company received more claims to review and thus stood to make a large amount of money in the review process; on the other hand, doctors whose reports did not help the insurer were dropped. As part of the strategy, any IME report that even remotely questioned the medical validity of the claim became the basis for denying the claim. The treating (claimant's) doctor's assessment was disregarded, and the claim was terminated. This allegation was made against other insurers as well but not with the same severity or frequency as against Provident. The company significantly beefed up its legal department to prepare for the lawsuits it knew were sure to follow. Doctors presenting an "independent" medical evaluation favorable to Provident were asked to testify on behalf of the company. Some IME doctors used by Provident spent as much time in the courtroom as they did in the examining room.

The "Hungry Vulture Award" and Its Impact on Claimants and Provident

In order to keep continuous pressure on Provident employees, Chandler held company assemblies and personally presented his creation, the "Hungry Vulture Award," which included not only a plaque but a cash bonus. According to allegations in many of the lawsuits filed against Provident, the Hungry Vulture Award was given to those employees who performed well—who happened to be the most aggressive in delaying, denying, and terminating Provident's disability claims. The award even carried the motto "Patience my foot . . . I'm gonna kill something." A Provident senior official denied the allegations of a link between aggressive claim management and receipt of the Hungry Vulture Award and stated that the award was only for exemplary performance, but other employees confirmed that the claims denial strategy came from top executives.[5]

The impact of these claim denials and abrupt termination of policyholders' benefits and claim payments caused economic chaos to those customers with legitimate disabilities. Chandler's plan struck when claimants were at their weakest—when they were disabled and least able to fight a major insurance company with millions of dollars and an army of lawyers.

Increased Claim Terminations

Chandler's strategy to boost Provident's bottom line was immediately successful. In 1995, just two years after Chandler came aboard, he was able to announce in Provident's Annual Report to Shareholders that the company had returned to profitability. In a surprisingly revealing statement in that report, Chandler cited "increased claim terminations" as the key factor in the recovery, and reported that "for every dollar we invested in claim management, this unit [the claims department] has returned up to $8 to the company."[6]

Chandler, key executives, and shareholders reaped the rewards of the strategy. Some key claims personnel received bonuses or other awards based on the number of claims terminated, and compensation packages were tied to bottom-line results. While it is not unusual to tie compensation or bonuses to profitability, and no one would disagree that invalid claims should be terminated, in case after case, attorneys proved in court that the company's policy was the termination of *valid*, payable claims. The words "increased claim terminations" tied to Provident's return to profitability in the company's annual report should have raised red flags to industry observers and state regulators, but no one seemed to notice the millions of dollars in claims that were routinely denied or terminated. Nor did regulators apparently react to the other red flag: Chandler's statement that investment in claims management brought a huge return to the company. Insurance regulators know the industry standard—insurance companies are not supposed to look to the claims department as a profit center—but the regulators did not react when these statements were made.

Chandler's aggressive claim termination policy eventually forced thousands of claimants and their families to give up any hope of a sustained fight against Provident. Many settled for pennies on the dollar, and many families never recovered.

During the next several years, Provident experienced a financial turnaround of major proportions. Millions of dollars came back into the Provident coffers. The company was now solidly in the black. Chandler walked on water in the eyes of the shareholders. Emboldened, he embarked on a series of mergers and acquisitions. These included the acquisition of the disability insurer Paul Revere Insurance Company of Boston in 1996 and a merger with another large disability carrier, Union Mutual (Unum) Insurance Company of Portland, Maine, in 1999. The company—now with a new corporate name, UnumProvident—became the largest individual and group disability insurer in the United States. In 1999, after the merger, UnumProvident boasted approximately 25 million policyholders nationwide.[7]

Policyholders Strike Back

In retrospect, it is clear that Chandler's "vulture" strategy was a serious error. The strategy almost imploded the company.

As word of the denials and terminations spread, many class action lawsuits and more than 4,000 other lawsuits were filed against the carrier, demanding compensatory and punitive damages. Although some cases had been filed earlier, Provident's litigation phase began in earnest in 1997. Some cases alleged securities fraud, while others alleged unfair competition, intentional bad faith, reckless claims handling, violations of state law, and fraudulent practices. The suits were filed from Maine to California.[8] The company vehemently denied all the allegations.

Former employees came forward, as did plaintiffs' attorneys who had seen the company's files in the course of litigation. They all made startling statements in depositions and at trial about the aggressive corporate culture. According to court records and media reports, they confirmed that managers kept a lid on costs by putting pressure on claims handlers and investigators to find any reason to deny large payouts. In depositions, some in-house company physicians said they felt pressured by managers to render the medical opinions needed to deny claims. In September 2002, one former in-house physician, Dr. Patrick F. McSharry, recalled in a deposition that one senior claims specialist routinely ran her finger across her neck in a slitting motion as she ordered staffers in claims review sessions to "close them down, get them off, get them out of here."[9]

Beginning in the late 1990s, as jury after jury heard these statements and the heart-wrenching tales of claimants whose legitimate disability claims were arbitrarily denied, multimillion-dollar judgments far in excess of actual damages were entered against the company as punishment for its reckless or malicious acts. The lawsuits against UnumProvident for bad faith (reckless claims handling) and breach of contract kept coming. There were still many outstanding cases against UnumProvident, and new filings continued in 2007.

Here are just a few examples of the million-dollar bad faith verdicts against UnumProvident:

■ John Tedesco was an eye surgeon with Parkinson's disease and a herniated disk. UnumProvident withheld his disability benefits. The insurance company took the position that Tedesco could still perform his occupation. A federal court in Florida awarded $36.7 million in favor of Tedesco against UnumProvident. To avoid a lengthy appeal, Tedesco settled with UnumProvident for an undisclosed sum.

■ Joanne Ceimo, a cardiologist, was permanently disabled after a neck injury caused trembling of her hand, preventing her from performing angioplasty and other delicate heart procedures. Yet her disability payments were cut off based on the opinions of three nontreating doctors who reported to UnumProvident that Ceimo might still be able to perform the procedures. The $84.5 million jury verdict against UnumProvident included $79 million in punitive damages against UnumProvident, which announced that it intended to file post-trial motions. On September 17, 2003, the trial court sustained the jury's decision to levy punitive damages against UnumProvident, but reduced the award from $79 million to $7 million. The remainder of the original verdict of $5.5 million was upheld by the court. In addition, the court awarded the plaintiff $600,000 in attorneys' fees.

■ Joan Hangartner, a veteran California chiropractor, experienced intense pain when doing spinal manipulations. UnumProvident nevertheless decided she was well enough to work in her specialty and abruptly cut off her benefits. The jury awarded Hangartner $7.6 million. Judge James Larson strongly rebuked UnumProvident for violating California's Unfair Business Practices Code. Judge Larson issued an injunction for the company to obey the law and enjoined it from future violations, including but not limited to targeting for termination categories of claims or claimants, employing biased medical examiners, destroying medical reports, and withholding from claimants information about their benefits.

■ Randall Chapman, a Novato, California, eye surgeon, developed a phobia just before his surgeries that caused his hand to shake violently during delicate eye procedures. UnumProvident called him a fraud and falsely claimed that he wasn't even an eye surgeon. In late January 2003, a California jury determined that UnumProvident had illegally cut off Chapman's benefits and awarded him $31.7 million, $30 million of which was punitive damages. UnumProvident filed post-trial motions, claiming the verdict was excessive. On March 25, 2003, the court entered an order reducing the punitive damage award to $5 million, thereby reducing the total award to $6.1 million. On April 8, 2003, the plaintiff accepted the reduced award.

■ Clinton Merrick was a sixty-one-year-old venture capitalist who was suffering from chronic fatigue syndrome, a condition that prevented him from traveling and doing analytical work. In December 2004, a federal jury in Las Vegas awarded him more than $11.1 million. The insurer stalled payments for eight years and finally denied his disability claim. The jury came down heavily on Unum-Provident's tactics. A major component of the award was $8 million in punitive damages against UnumProvident, the parent company, and a $2 million punitive damage award against Paul Revere Insurance Company (Unum's subsidiary, the actual writer of the policy).

And the list of cases goes on and on.[10]

Some plaintiffs felt it was so important to expose UnumProvident's actions that they chose to go forward with their suits in part to alert the public to the inadequate regulation by the state insurance departments. Joanne Ceimo, for example, announced plans to donate half her damages award to charity and said, "This was never about the money. It was always about stopping these insurance companies from intentionally hurting people."[11]

By awarding such huge sums against UnumProvident, juries have validated the importance of jury trials. In these cases, average citizens stepped into a regulatory void and became a force for good—for the industry, as well as for consumers—and juries sent a message to the insurance industry that it must honor its own time-honored industry commandments:

1. The company shall always remember that an insurance claims department is not supposed to be a profit center.
2. The company shall not create incentives for termination of legitimate claims as a way to increase or restore its profitability.
3. The company shall treat an insured's interests with the same regard as it does its own interests.
4. The company shall not make insurance an adversarial process.

While these principles are not codified in law or regulation, they are critical components of the insurance product.

The Media and the Regulators Weigh In

In May 2002, *Forbes* magazine named Chandler the third worst CEO in America.[12] In late 2002, UnumProvident's problems grew into a public relations nightmare when reporters from CBS-TV's *60 Minutes* and NBC-TV's *Dateline NBC* revealed the insurance company's abuses and leveled serious allegations of fraud. In addition to presenting a critical analysis of UnumProvident's attempt to solve its financial difficulties by refusing to pay legitimate claims, *60 Minutes* and *Dateline NBC* offered compelling interviews with claimants who were the victims of this practice.

One of the most gripping statements came not from a victim but from the newly reelected California insurance commissioner, John Garamendi, on *60 Minutes*. The commissioner told anchor Ed Bradley that UnumProvident's adjusters appeared to be under pressure to increase the number of claim terminations, an action that could "lead to fraud by the insurance company against the consumer, against the policyholder." It was, he said, "a clear siren out in the street, saying, what is going on here?" Garamendi told the TV audience that the company's business strategy might have gone something like this: "How many [lawsuits and how much business] will we lose, versus how much will we gain by denying these claims?" In addition, he conjectured, Unum may have thought, "probably the departments of insurance are asleep anyway, so let's go."

Outrage was so great from the public against the company and Chandler's policies that UnumProvident took the unusual step of publishing full-page informational advertisements in major newspapers and began a public relations campaign to blunt the charges. On October 14, 2002, Chandler wrote to "friends of UnumProvident" rebutting *Dateline NBC*'s exposé, and on November 18, 2002, Tom Watjen, UnumProvident's chief operating officer, issued a similar rebuttal to the *60 Minutes* exposé. The programs stood by their stories.[13]

In general, Wall Street was late to advise the public about what was happening at UnumProvident. For example, analysts at a well-known brokerage house failed to lower their ratings on UnumProvident stock despite the mounting news about the company. They were aware that their company was underwriting bonds for UnumProvident and were afraid of the impact a negative review would have on the offering. This was a questionable if not unethical conflict of interest. When the analysts finally lowered the company's rating, it was too late. The stock value had dropped precipitously, and shareholders became unnerved. Investors, who initially saw their stock climb to over $50 per share after the Unum and Provident merger in 1999, watched helplessly as the stock sank to $14.45 per share on February 6, 2003. UnumProvident had become the worst performer on the Standard & Poor's 500 Insurance Index.[14]

On the regulatory front, Georgia State Insurance Commissioner John Oxendine reported in early 2003 that UnumProvident's corporate mentality included "looking for every technical legal way to avoid paying a claim." By February 2003, state insurance regulators were alarmed. In the middle of March 2003, Georgia insurance officials concluded their investigation of UnumProvident. They levied a fine of $1 million related to claims handling and put the company on probation for two years. This was the largest fine the state of Georgia had ever levied against an insurer.

In December 2003, *Business Week* reported that forty-five states were jointly investigating the way UnumProvident handled claims. This was the largest investigation of an insurance company ever undertaken in the United States.[15]

Exit Chandler

The bad news about UnumProvident, once just a murmur in the insurance world, became a loud roar in 2003. In rapid succession, the company was battered from all sides.

- The SEC forced UnumProvident to restate three years of earnings and to resolve issues raised by the regulators.

- A court in California entered a jury verdict of millions of dollars in punitive damages against it for bad faith reckless claims handling.

- Class action lawsuits alleged the company was running claim-denial factories.

- Other states initiated investigations into the company's practices.

The problems didn't stop there. UnumProvident's stock continued to decline, reaching a low of $6 per share several months later.[16]

In an apparent response to what was characterized as a whirlwind of legal, regulatory, and media attacks, and a continual stream of bad news, the UnumProvident board announced on March 31, 2003, that it had fired J. Harold Chandler as chairman, chief executive officer, and president of the company.[17] By this time, Chandler had been at the helm of the company for almost ten years.

The once all-powerful Chandler was unavailable for comment on the day of the firing. Still, he may have had the last laugh: Chandler walked away with approximately $17 million—$8.5 million in severance pay and $8.5 million in pension benefits. One year after he left the company, Chandler sued UnumProvident, seeking final payment under his employment contract. He received an additional $2.9 million, the full amount under his contract.[18]

The Regulatory Settlement Agreement

In 2004, largely as a result of the climate created by Chandler's vulture culture, and after intense investigation, UnumProvident was forced to enter into a major settlement with state regulators. Forty states signed the agreement. UnumProvident agreed to set aside more than $113 million to pay previously denied claims, to pay a fine of $15 million, and to review and reassess more than 200,000 denied or terminated claims dating back to 1997.[19]

This multistate regulatory action against UnumProvident was vindication for some. But to many others representing policyholders—such as veteran litigation attorneys Eugene Anderson in New York and Ray Bourhis in San Francisco, and well-respected industry observer Joseph Belth, an insurance professor emeritus at Indiana University—the settlement failed to solve one of the main underlying problems: improper regulation.

Anderson, Bourhis, and Belth are well known to the courts, the regulators, and the insurance industry as observers of the industry and fighters for the insurance consumer.[20] They argued that the settlement was woefully inadequate, in that money paid by UnumProvident was too little, too late; that many claims (those filed before 1997) were left out of the review pool; and that UnumProvident should not have been allowed to select the panel reviewing the claims. Most important, the critics believed that the regulators should have made UnumProvident admit that the company was engaging in unfair claim settlement practices, which the regulators did not do. Notwithstanding the efforts of these men and many other spokespersons for policyholders, the regulators carried out the settlement with the carrier. At the end of the day, UnumProvident admitted no liability, made no apology, and walked away, monetarily, relatively unscathed.

J. Harold Chandler, chief executive and the architect of the Hungry Vulture Award, was gone from the UnumProvident insurance scene.[21] In Chandler's wake were the ruined lives of hundreds, maybe thousands, of claimants with legitimate financial needs, who had paid their premiums but were denied the benefits on which they expected to live and support their families. Investors and employees were also badly hurt.

The element of trust, the cornerstone of insurance, was destroyed by Chandler's regime. In the years since his departure in 2003, the new executives at UnumProvident have been trying to restore that trust, but they have had a major public relations job on their hands. The new CEO, Tom Watjen—a key executive on Chandler's watch—has attempted to distance himself from the former CEO's malfeasance. In the January 2006 edition of *Insurance Journal*, Watjen was quoted as saying, "UnumProvident had been cleansed of the 'arrogance' brought about by market dominance. It was very much a top-down, 'don't really care what the employees think' attitude."[22]

As to Chandler, he joined with other investors to buy the benefits enrollment firm Turner P. Williams & Associates of Nashville a short time after leaving UnumProvident. The company became Benefit Partners of America, a worksite-marketing firm that designed, marketed, and administered voluntary insurance programs via payroll deduction for large U.S. employers. Chandler assumed the post of chairman and CEO. The following year, USI Holdings Corp. of Briarcliff Manor, N.Y., acquired Benefit Partners. Terms of the deal weren't disclosed, but according to a press release at the time, the acquisition was expected to add approximately $4 million in annual revenues to USI. Chandler was named director of strategic development.[23] The company has since been renamed Univers Workplace Benefits, with Chandler serving as the COO.

A Failure to Regulate
Martin Frankel, Liberty National

Some have called Martin Frankel the greatest con artist the United States ever knew.[24] He certainly was a master manipulator and one of the biggest insurance rogue executives to come along in years. He made front-page headlines and became the lightning rod for a Government Accountability Office (GAO) study on what was wrong with insurance regulation.[25]

In 1991, Frankel—already under investigation by the SEC in 1989 for fraudulent activities (omissions and misstatements to investors about his investment practices)—slipped under the radar and quietly acquired Franklin American Life Insurance Co., and, within the next few years, seven other small life insurance companies. The companies operated primarily in six states in the rural South under the umbrella name of Thunor Trust, headquartered in Tennessee.[26] The companies mainly sold inexpensive insurance to poor farmers who paid minimal amounts each week to pay for their burial costs.

Before allowing Frankel to acquire the insurance companies in 1991, no one in Tennessee or in any other state checked Frankel's prior record. Had they done so, they would have found that Frankel was banned for life by the SEC in 1992 for the fraudulent activities for which he was investigated starting in 1989. In addition, they did not notice that after his acquisition of the insurance companies, Frankel had plenty of cash and luxury cars, had acquired two mansions in posh Greenwich, Connecticut, and in general was living lavishly.

Over an eight-year period, Frankel looted the companies, right under the nose of the state insurance regulators throughout the South. How did he do it? The scheme was simple. Frankel applied to the Tennessee state securities department for a license under the name of Liberty National Securities, and to the Tennessee Department of Commerce and Insurance for insurance regulatory approval for Thunor Trust. Frankel's name was never used in those applications or in subsequent communications; he operated by using aliases or through fronts. No one ever checked the veracity of the information supplied.

Liberty National was supposed to invest money for the insurers. Instead, Frankel, the CEO of all of the insurance companies and the CEO of Liberty National, transferred the Thunor Trust assets (the millions of dollars of cash held by Thunor Trust for the eight insurance companies) into Liberty National. He then moved the money out of Liberty National and put it into a number of untraceable accounts, presumably for his own use, leaving Thunor Trust and the insurance companies with no money. In 1999, more than $200 million was gone from Liberty National. Frankel's insurance companies had been stripped of their funds, leaving policyholders with worthless policies.

Realizing that he was being sought by police in various states, Frankel fled to Europe, taking with him suitcases filled with diamonds valued at more than $10 million. In Europe, he started a new anonymous life and led U.S. authorities and Interpol on a search around the globe. In September 1999, he was apprehended in Germany by Interpol and extradited to the United States for trial in a federal court. Frankel could have faced a sentence of up to 150 years and $6.5 million in fines. Instead, he pleaded guilty and was sentenced to sixteen years for looting and bankrupting the life insurance companies. He is currently in a federal prison in Texas.

In addition to the federal criminal charges levied against Frankel (wire fraud, money laundering, securities fraud, racketeering, and conspiracy to commit racketeering), he also faced fraud charges from the SEC and fraud and embezzlement charges ($200 million) from five states (Arkansas, Mississippi, Missouri, Oklahoma, and Tennessee).[27] The missing millions stolen by Frankel will most likely never be recovered.

Turning a Blind Eye

How did Frankel manage to steal so much money and get away with his scheme? Initially, Frankel obtained public investor money and approval in the business community by misrepresenting the identity of his financial sources and backing for the insurance acquisition. In addition to filing applications to the states under false names, Frankel, under false pretenses, received an affidavit from a Vatican official stating that he was active in Catholic philanthropy and that he had a legitimate insurance business. The seeming endorsement by the Vatican gave him the stamp of approval he needed in the business community.

The Frankel story attracted major media coverage, not only because of the amount of money stolen (at one time the estimate was as high as $3 billion, but the number has since been revised downward to $200 million), but because of the way Frankel's companies and his questionable practices went unnoticed, or ignored, by the state insurance regulators. Regulators in several of the states came under fire for not heeding red flags that critics say should have signaled problems long before they were noticed. One of these signals was highly unusual trading volume that sometimes amounted to assets being turned over one hundred times in a year. When suspicions finally were raised, the regulators didn't share their concerns. As Deborah Lohse reported in the *Wall Street Journal*, "the skirmishing [as to which state guaranty fund will pay the insurance claims due to the insolvency of Frankel's insurance companies] could fur-

ther highlight the shortfalls in the system of state insurance regulation."[28]

The Tennessee Connection

The majority of Frankel's companies were domiciled (incorporated
in the state) in Tennessee, an insurance industry–friendly state. For
example, after the theft was discovered, the GAO reported that Tennessee state auditors notified the Tennessee insurance commissioner,
Douglas Sizemore, early on that they thought there were discrepanc-
ies and that money was missing from Frankel's companies, but
Sizemore did nothing.[29]

The Frankel probe eventually forced the Tennessee Bureau of
Investigation to seize the files of Frankel's insurance companies.
Shortly thereafter, Insurance Commissioner Sizemore resigned.[30]
According to press accounts, Sizemore's son was doing business with
Frankel.[31] The governor of Tennessee said that while there was the
appearance of linkage between the Frankel episode and Sizemore's
resignation, it was never confirmed. No formal accusations of
wrongdoing were made about Sizemore or his son.

The Aftermath: The Failure of the Regulators Exposed

This entire episode revealed the "gaping holes in the states' regulatory net," as *New York Times* reporter Joseph Kahn characterized
it.[32] The *Times* article voiced what has become a common view, that
". . . the Frankel case has added momentum to those who argue that
state autonomy in insurance regulation is outdated. At a minimum,
the fraud and intense coverage it has received seem likely to add
pressure on states to improve oversight or risk losing some authority, government and industry leaders said."[33]

Insurance guaranty fund administrators in forty-one states have been cleaning up after Frankel, and serious attention is now being given to "how to prevent another scam of this caliber."[34]

In March 2000, after reports of the Frankel fraud blanketed the media, the National Association of Insurance Commissioners, in an unusual move, revoked the Tennessee Department of Insurance of accreditation. The NAIC claimed that the department did a poor job of detecting the insurance fraud committed by Frankel. The accreditation was reinstated six months later.[35]

Meanwhile, in a remarkably brazen and non-remorseful television interview on ABC-TV's *20/20* in May 2000, Frankel dismissed his actions as mere "financial crimes," implying that that type of crime did no harm to anyone.[36]

In fact, everyone suffers from actions like Frankel's. Any time state guaranty funds are used to pay the obligations of a bankrupt insurer, the other carriers in the affected state are assessed a payment proportional to their revenue generated in that state. The assessed insurers, in turn, pass along the cost to their customers through increased premiums, decreased benefits, or both. Furthermore, although state insurance guaranty funds will pay for some of the policyholders' claims, most states have limits on how much can be paid ($100,000 to $300,000 maximum per claim), and there is always the danger that the funds may run out of cash under pressure of too many claims or because the funds themselves are underfunded.

Inadequate Oversight
Saul Steinberg, Reliance Insurance Company

In 1968, at the age of twenty-nine, Saul Steinberg acquired the Philadelphia-based Reliance Insurance Company in a leveraged buyout. The 150-year-old company with a stodgy reputation was being taken over by a brash young entrepreneur. Eyebrows rose all over the insurance world. Could the new leader make it work?

At the time, Steinberg was known as a young man who had been a brilliant student at the Wharton School, the University of Pennsylvania's business school, and had been able to leverage his fledgling company (Leasco, which leased IBM computers to businesses) into a powerhouse. With stock from Leasco, he acquired Reliance, primarily a property and casualty insurance company. Under Steinberg's tutelage as chairman of the board, Reliance was always on the prowl for bigger and more interesting risks, in order to make more money for the shareholders—which, of course, included Steinberg, one of the largest shareholders.

With the money pouring in to Reliance, Steinberg was on a roll. Along with the money came lavish art collections, homes, society parties, and major philanthropy. Steinberg's open checkbook was well known and he became a celebrity. For example, he donated millions to remodel and reface Wharton's old Dietrich Hall on the University of Pennsylvania campus, and the name on the building was changed to Steinberg Hall-Dietrich Hall. A picture of philanthropist and alumnus Saul Steinberg still hangs in the building's entrance hall.

Steinberg amassed a fortune, which once topped $600 million. From 1982 to 1995, he was on *Forbes'* list of the 400 Richest Americans. He operated under the umbrella organization Reliance Group Holdings, Inc. As the years went by, the pressure for greater cash flow increased, and Reliance began to write policies with lower and lower premiums and higher and higher risk. While Reliance cornered a large segment of the market, the big property and casualty insurer was heading for financial trouble.

By the late 1990s, rumors began to surface that Reliance was weak and going under. Great numbers of policies were being written, but reserves for claims were not sufficient. A clue to how serious the problems were began to emerge as Steinberg began auctioning off millions of dollars' worth of art. Around the same time, Steinberg's mother sued him and his brother Robert for failure to repay a $6 million note (Robert, also an executive, had a subsidiary role in Reliance). Almost unnoticed, but most significant, claim payments by Reliance were slowing down.

In the spring of 2001, Reliance shocked the insurance world when it collapsed financially. The insurer was placed into rehabilitation by Pennsylvania Insurance Commissioner Diane Koken, for what was characterized by the commissioner as a "declining capital position." Shortly thereafter, in October 2001, seeing no hope for a turnaround, the commissioner ordered that Reliance be liquidated, and she took on the role of liquidator on behalf of the Commonwealth of Pennsylvania. At the time, it was estimated that Reliance had a cash shortfall of more than $1 billion and was unable to pay its claims and its creditors.

In late 2001, veteran *Philadelphia Inquirer* business and insurance reporter Joseph N. DiStefano wrote an in-depth five-part series on the fall of Reliance and Steinberg. DiStefano projected this to be the largest insurance company failure in history, and he was right.[37] By 2004, Reliance's loss had grown to approximately $3 billion, much more than was estimated in 2001.[38]

Investigations under the direction of the Pennsylvania Insurance Department raised serious questions about Saul Steinberg. In December 2001, the *Philadelphia Inquirer* reported that the Commonwealth of Pennsylvania was preparing to sue Reliance officers and managers, including Steinberg, in an attempt to recoup the funds allegedly improperly removed from Reliance.[39] The investigation culminated in a major federal suit filed against Steinberg and other senior executives.

The complaint filed by Commissioner Koken, as liquidator of Reliance on behalf of Pennsylvania, alleged that Steinberg, together with other high-ranking executives, had extracted hundreds of millions of dollars from Reliance before the company was placed in liquidation by the Pennsylvania Insurance Department. The executives were charged with draining cash from the company to support their lavish lifestyles.[40]

The allegations against Steinberg and other top Reliance officials included the charge that the defendants permitted $500 million in cash to be diverted from the insurer Reliance to the parent companies in the form of dividends, bogus tax payments, and loans. The complaint went on to say that Reliance directors and officers:

> ... knew or should have known that the lavish lifestyles of controlling shareholders, including defendant Saul Steinberg, the enormous debt of the parent holding companies, and the huge personal debt of Saul Steinberg, had become the driving force behind the draining of Reliance's cash, rather than the best interests of the company and its policyholders.[41]

The complaint went further. It alleged that "Defendants' relentless bleeding of cash and surplus from Reliance during the precise period when defendants knew or should have known that reserves were understated . . . broke the back of the company and caused it to crumble and fail."

The lawsuit accused the defendants of rewarding executives with excessive salaries and bonuses, even as the company slipped into insolvency, and of misusing corporate property; for example, 55 percent of the trips on the company's five-bedroom private jet were personal trips made by Saul Steinberg and his brother. In 2000 and 2001, the period in which the company became insolvent, Reliance paid $7 million to Robert Steinberg in lump salary and termination-settlement payments.

Steinberg and the other key former Reliance executives agreed in February 2005 to pay $51 million—a far cry from the $3 billion shortfall owed to claimants and creditors—to the Commonwealth of Pennsylvania in settlement of all claims against them. As part of this settlement, Robert Steinberg returned the $7 million that had been paid to him.[42]

Some of the viable parts of Reliance's business were picked up by other insurance companies; however, there is little hope of a full repayment of amounts owed to policyholders. It certainly will not be repaid through the limited resources of the state insurance guaranty fund. Litigation continues.

Most disconcerting is that the Pennsylvania Department of Insurance, which was supposed to guard the interests of policyholders, did not act in time to rehabilitate the company because it was unaware of the depth of the problems at Reliance. The department discovered the financial crisis only in the year 2000, after Reliance filed its 1999 annual report to the Commonwealth. The report, when analyzed by the department, was a surprise. It showed that Reliance could not meet the state Insurance Department solvency tests. The state then tried to move swiftly to attempt to rehabilitate Reliance, but it was too late. By the year 2001, Reliance, one of the major property and casualty insurers in the United States, which had been founded in 1817, had ceased to exist as a functioning insurance company.

In late 2004, it was reported that Steinberg, once a shining star, was an ill and broken man. He is currently living in New York.

The Steinberg/Reliance story underscores the hazy legal regulatory climate in which the insurance industry has been operating and the devastating effect it has had on many claimants, creditors, employees, and the general business community. The problem may not have been solely within the Pennsylvania Department of Insurance.

Once Commissioner Koken learned of the problem with Reliance, she moved swiftly to attempt to put the company into rehabilitation. When rehabilitation failed and she had to put Reliance into liquidation, Koken moved forcefully and hired effective counsel to root out the wrongdoing at Reliance.[43] She also kept the public informed. With twenty-twenty hindsight, if the Pennsylvania Department of Insurance had a bigger budget and more personnel, and/or if they had the opportunity to observe Steinberg and Reliance earlier and more closely (Pennsylvania does a full in-house audit of insurers only once every three to five years), they might have been able to protect against this financial disaster.

■ ■ ■

The Chandler, Frankel, and Steinberg stories are perfect examples of failures of executive accountability and failures of the regulators. In each case, it was not until well after the damage was done that action was taken against the individuals. By then, it was too late for the company, employees, stockholders, claimants, creditors, regulators, and the public. They all lost.

Notes

1. All of the details were taken from complaints and industry observations; see, for example, *Giarraputo et al. v. UnumProvident Corp., et al.* (USDC, District of Maine, Case Number 2: 99cv 00301—SJM) filed September 30, 1999, a class action suit alleging securities fraud. See also *United Policyholders and Evans v. Provident Life and Accident*, Alameda County (Oakland), California, filed August 13, 1999, which alleges a violation of California's Unfair Competition Act. All of the cases resulted in substantial monetary awards against Unum-Provident or settlements by UnumProvident. The Giarraputo et al. case was settled for $45 million, and a settlement order was entered by the USDC, District of Maine, on July 12, 2004. The United Policyholders and Evans case had a large verdict against UnumProvident; see Dean Foust, Anand Natarajan, and Brian Grow, "Disability Claim Denied!" *Business Week,* December 22, 2003, pp. 62–63, available at http://www.businessweek.com/magazine/con tent/03_51/b3863104_mz020.htm; see also cases cited below.
2. Provident Life and Accident, Annual Report, 1993.
3. See Note 1 above and Notes 10, 11, and 12 below.
4. Foust, Natarajan, and Grow, "Disability Claim Denied!" See also cases cited throughout these notes.
5. According to *Business Week*, after Provident merged with Unum in 1999, Linda Nee, a veteran claims handler, and other employees at Unum's head

office in Portland, Maine, said they started seeing a more ruthless approach to claims. The pressure peaked, they say, in the last month of each quarter—the "scrub months," when managers looked for claims to terminate to get under budget. The company vigorously denied that it rejected claims for financial reasons and said that Nee was fired in 2002 for poor performance. Nee, who worked for Unum for eight years, confirmed that she was terminated, but she said it was because she was a whistleblower. See Foust, Natarajan, and Grow, "Disability Claim Denied!" For the comment by the Provident official defending the company's action, see http://www.businessweek.com/magazine/content/03_51/b3863104_mz020.htm.

6. UnumProvident, Annual Report, 1995.

7. UnumProvident records.

8. See Note 1 above and Notes 10, 11, and 12 below.

9. Foust, Natarajan, and Grow, "Disability Claim Denied!"

10. *Chapman v. UnumProvident* (California State Court, San Raphael, California), January 2003. See also *Hangartner v. UnumProvident* (USDC, San Francisco), 2002. For more about UnumProvident cases, see Michael Liedtke, Associated Press, "Suing the Vulture," December 15, 2002, available at http://64.233.169 .104/search?q = cache:MFyHoDe_KtYJ:www.miraclemakersclub.com/ha_arti cle_3.htm + Michael + Liedtke, + %E2%80%9CSuing + the + Vulture,%E2% 80%9D + Associated + Press, + December + 15, + 2002&hl = en&ct = clnk&cd = 1&gl = us].

11. Liedtke, "Suing the Vulture."

12. *Forbes,* May 2002, p. 112, available at http://members.forbes.com/forbes/2002/0513/112tab.html.

13. *Dateline NBC*, October 13, 2002; *60 Minutes* (CBS), November 17, 2002, Ed Bradley, anchor.

14. David Plumb, "UnumProvident Shares Fall on Earnings, SEC Review," Blomberg.com, February 6, 2003.

15. Foust, Natarajan, and Grow, "Disability Claim Denied!"; see also Christopher Oster, "Jury Rules UnumProvident Acted With Fraud, Malice," *Wall Street Journal*, January 27, 2003.

16. Standard & Poor's records.

17. Christopher Oster, "UnumProvident Fires Chandler as CEO, Names Interim Chief," *Wall Street Journal,* April 1, 2003.

18. *Chandler v. UnumProvident* (Tennessee State Court), March 5, 2003.

19. UnumProvident multistate Settlement Agreement, November 18, 2004.

20. Eugene Anderson is a former federal prosecutor and currently a civil litigator in New York. He, together with other members of his law firm, has won a

significant number of lawsuits against insurance carriers. Anderson was dubbed "dean of policyholders" by *Business Week*. Ray Bourhis has won several multimillion-dollar bad faith suits against insurers for reckless claims handling. He is the author of *Insult to Injury: Insurance, Fraud, and the Big Business of Bad Faith* (San Francisco: Berrett-Koehler Publishers, 2005), a powerful, heartfelt book that focused on one of his cases against UnumProvident, in which he won a substantial verdict. In the book he described Unum-Provident's claim denial tactics through his eyes and through evidence introduced at trial, as well as other information. He also described the devastating impact the claim denial had on his client. Joseph M. Belth, Ph.D., is professor emeritus of insurance in the Kelley School of Business at Indiana University (Bloomington), editor of *The Insurance Forum*, an informative and insightful regular newsletter publication, and author of *Life Insurance: A Consumer's Handbook*.

21. Drew Ruble, ed., "Vestige of Empire," *Business TN Magazine*, July 31, 2006, http://www.businesstn.com/pub/3_7/cover/7931–1.html.

22. *Insurance Journal*, January 2006; see also Ruble, "Vestige of Empire," http://www.insurancejournal.com/magazines/east/2006/01/02/features/64529.html.

23. Ruble, "Vestige of Empire."

24. Many in the media called Frankel a con man; see, for example, Associated Press, "Ex-financier Frankel Indicted on 36 Counts," October 7, 1999; "Tennessee Comptroller Seizes Franklin American Files from Insurance Commissioner," Insure.com; Deborah Lohse and Leslie Scism, "How Frankel Created an Insurance Empire," *Wall Street Journal*, July 2, 1999; Denise Lavoie, "Financier, $3B in Clients' Funds Missing since May 5," Associated Press, June 23, 1999. Frankel also was the subject of Ellen Joan Pollock, *The Pretender: How Martin Frankel Fooled the Financial World and Led the Feds on One of the Most Publicized Manhunts in History* (New York: Free Press, 2002), as well as other books and magazine articles. An exposé of him by Brian Ross aired on May 13, 2000, on ABC-TV's *20/20*.

25. Ibid. See also Richard J. Hillman, "Insurance Regulation: Scandal Highlights Need for States to Strengthen Regulatory Oversight," testimony before the House Subcommittee on Finance and Hazardous Materials, Committee on Commerce, September 19, 2000, GAO/T-GGD-00–209. Hillman is the associate director of Financial Institutions and Market Issues, General Government Division, Government Accountability Office.

26. Frankel owned a total of nine companies, eight of which were insurance companies: Old Southwest Life (Arkansas); Franklin Protective Life Insurance Co., Family Guaranty Life Insurance Co., and First National Life Co. of America

(all in Mississippi); International Services Life Insurance Co. (Missouri); Farmers and Ranchers Life Insurance Co. (Oklahoma); Franklin American Life Insurance Co. (Tennessee); and Settlers Life Insurance Co. (Virginia). The ninth company, Liberty National Securities Inc., the investment company, was based in Greenwich, Connecticut. The regulators failed to note that Frankel was banned for life by the SEC in 1992.

27. Mark Cybulski, "SEC Sues Frankel for Embezzling Money from Life Insurers," Insure.com, September 28, 2000; Mark Cybulski, "Five State Insurance Departments Sue Martin Frankel for $200 Million," Insure.com, March 16, 2000.

28. Deborah Lohse, "Frankel Case: Insurers Spar Over Funds," *Wall Street Journal*, July 7, 1999.

29. Roger Hillman, "The NAIC Accreditation Program Can Be Improved," report to the Honorable John D. Dingell, Committee on Energy and Commerce, House of Representatives, August 2001, GAO-01–948, http://www.gao.gov/new.items/d01948.pdf.

30. Scott J. Paltrow, "Tennessee Insurance Official Quits Amid Frankel-Related Inquiry," *Wall Street Journal, Interactive Edition*, August 9, 1999.

31. Paltrow, "Tennessee Insurance Official Quits."

32. Joseph Kahn, "Insurance Fraud Shows Gaping Holes in the States' Regulatory Net," *New York Times*, July 6, 1999.

33. Kahn, "Insurance Fraud Shows Gaping Holes."

34. Theresa Miller, "Vehicle for a Swindle," *Best's Review Life/Health*, September 1999.

35. Mark Cybulski, "Accreditation Yanked from Tennessee Insurance Department," Insure.com, March 30, 2000; Mark Cybulski, "Tennessee Insurance Department Regains Accreditation," Insure.com, September 14, 2000.

36. Interview with Martin Frankel, *20/20*, ABC-TV, May 13, 2000.

37. Joseph N. DiStefano, "The Empire Builders," *The Philadelphia Inquirer Magazine*, December 9, 2001. Although the Reliance liquidation was the largest in history, it is by no means the only insolvency with which states are dealing. By 2004, the Pennsylvania Insurance Department listed twenty-two companies (including Reliance) considered domiciled in Pennsylvania as "currently in liquidation." Some of these liquidations were started as early as 1984, and many long-time insolvent carriers are still listed as being liquidated.

38. Joseph DiStefano, "PA Tries to Recoup Reliance Expenses," *Philadelphia Inquirer*, June 1, 2004, Business Section, p. C1.

39. "PA Prepares to Sue Reliance Officers," *Philadelphia Inquirer*, December 18, 2001.

40. "Pennsylvania Insurance Dept Investigating Removal of Hundreds of Millions of Dollars from Reliance," *Philadelphia Inquirer*, November 30, 2001.

41. Pennsylvania Insurance Commissioner Koken filed a malpractice lawsuit in Pennsylvania's Commonwealth Court against Reliance's former auditor and outside actuary, Deloitte & Touche LLP, and one of its principals. The Pennsylvania Insurance Department blamed Deloitte & Touche and its principal actuary for inflating Reliance's financial statements by $1 billion and contributing to its financial collapse in 2001. It was alleged that Deloitte & Touche understated the company's expected insurance claims by more than $500 million and exaggerated assets by $500 million. See Joseph N. DiStefano, *Philadelphia Inquirer*, October 17, 2002.

42. Ibid., DiStefano, *Philadelphia Inquirer*, October 17, 2002.

43. "PA Will Close, Not Reorganize, Phila Insurer: Reliance Will Be Unable to Pay Some of its $10 Billion in Liabilities, State Insurance Commissioner Diane Koken Said," *Philadelphia Inquirer*, October 4, 2001.

Cartoon by J. D. Crowe, *Mobile Register*, Mobile, Alabama 2006. Reprinted with permission of artist.

CHAPTER 3

How the Industry Got Where It Is Today
Unpaid Claims and the Storm after Hurricane Katrina

"The people of the area that have been damaged by Hurricane Katrina cannot wait any longer [to have their claims paid]. And I expect this to be done momentarily. And, if it's not, there's going to be hell to pay. . . ."

Senator Trent Lott (R, Mississippi), February 10, 2006

"Since Hurricane Katrina—which caused a record $50 billion in insured losses—private insurers have jacked up premiums as much as they can. And, when barred from raising prices, dropped coverage of riskier homes. Many of these companies, which have turned denying valid claims into an art form, deserve little sympathy. . . ."

—"Insurance for the Next Big One," *New York Times* editorial,
October 1, 2007

"Claim Denied . . . Denied . . . Denied"

More than any other event in recent memory, the denial of hundreds of thousands of Hurricane Katrina–related homeowners and business insurance claims, estimated at $2 billion, touched a nerve with the U.S. public. The insurers based the nonpayment on a "gotcha clause" in the insurance policy. If you were a policyholder insured for hurricane damage, whose home, business, or auto was damaged by *only* hurricane winds, you were covered. However, if your home, business, or auto was damaged by a combination of hurricane wind *and* floodwater, you were not covered. The small print in the policy said that damage by "wind and water" together was not covered.

On March 1, 2007, Robert P. Hartwig, president of the Insurance Information Institute, the information arm of the insurance industry, testified before the House Financial Services Subcommittee on Oversight and Investigations that the industry had paid more than $40 billion in Katrina claims. This represented 1.7 million claims for damage to homes, businesses, and vehicles in six states—the largest loss by far in the history of insurance, dwarfing the total paid out as a result of Hurricane Andrew in 1992. He further stated that 95 percent of the 1.1 million homeowners insurance claims in Louisiana and Mississippi—totaling more than $15.5 billion—were settled within one year of the storm. Hartwig also estimated that fewer than 2 percent of homeowner, business, and auto claims in Mississippi and Louisiana were in dispute through either mediation or litigation.

When questioned by Representative Maxine Waters (D, California), Hartwig admitted that the 95 percent figure did not include claims the insurers asserted were barred by language in the policies—that is, policies that included the "wind and water" language.

The attorney general of Mississippi, Jim Hood, estimated that at least 5 percent of the $40 billion remained unpaid, and sued the insurers on behalf of the citizens of Mississippi to recover $2 billion.

Flood Damage vs. Wind Damage

The anti-concurrent causation clause, as the wind and water clause is known in the insurance industry, is one of those insurance clauses that is hardly ever noticed by the consumer, and, if noticed, is often not understood. As a result, in addition to the normal skirmishes between claimant and insurer as to the valuation of claims, the wind versus water issue added a major new dimension when its implementation resulted in massive denials, outrage among policyholders, and at least one insensitive comment by an industry representative who advised the public to "read your policy."[1]

Insurance industry representatives argue that without the anti-concurrent causation language, insurers could not limit their liability and would be subject to pressure to pay claims that they normally would not pay. The clause, they say, tries to make the policy clear. Policyholders argue that the clause is a perfect example of a "gotcha" provision, with its legalistic language that slips by the consumer and that the insurer does not explain. In effect, policyholders argue, the clauses eliminate the very coverage that insurers appear to be promising when they sell the policies.

If the devastation Katrina caused was the result of a combination of wind and flood, it leaves a legal gray area and fertile ground for litigation. As a result, there have been a large number of lawsuits, protracted litigation, trials, and settlement negotiations, all of which resulted in delay, which in turn created economic and financial pressure.

The "Exhibit 1" gray area is New Orleans, Louisiana, a city built on ground several feet below sea level. A major cause of the damage there was the rupture of the reinforced levies that held back the seawater. More than 200,000 homes and thousands of businesses were damaged or destroyed by the flooding. Was the cause flood, wind, or both?

Although homeowners' policies covered wind damage, insurers contended that the main cause of the devastation, loss of life, and property damage during Katrina was not caused by wind but by flood, which was not covered. As a result, hundreds of thousands of claims were not paid, and many people were forced to live in makeshift quarters, without work, without money, and unable to rebuild their lives.[2]

Katrina was the largest U.S. natural disaster in history. At times a Category 5 hurricane with 150 mph winds, Katrina struck the Gulf Coast on August 29, 2005, causing widespread death and damage in six southern states (Louisiana, Mississippi, Alabama, Florida, Tennessee, and Georgia): 1,836 dead, thousands injured, businesses ruined, families displaced, and 80 percent of New Orleans under water. Two years later, much of the area had not been rebuilt. As of August 2007, none of the 115 "critical priority projects" identified by city officials (such as police and fire facilities) had been completed. Total economic loss from homes, businesses, infrastructure, property damage, injuries, and death has been estimated at $125 billion, and insured losses from Katrina at $40 billion to $60 billion. More than 3 million insurance claims were filed.[3]

The Broussards Bring Suit Against State Farm

Like thousands of other homeowners, senior citizens Norman and Genevieve Broussard of Biloxi, Mississippi, believed their homeowners insurance policy covered hurricane damage. After Katrina hit, the Broussards filed their claim with State Farm Insurance, stating that their home was leveled by Katrina's hurricane-force winds, which caused a tornado, which was followed by flooding. The amount of their claim was modest: dwelling, $118,100, and contents, $88,575. They expected prompt payment. They were outraged when their claim was denied.

State Farm, the largest home insurer in Mississippi, told the Broussards that the damage to their home came from a water-related storm surge. State Farm reminded the Broussards that their homeowners' policy covered damage from wind, but excluded damage from water. The insurer said that the federal government—not private insurers—offered specialized flood insurance, which was available under a separate policy. The Broussards were out of luck.

This same scene occurred countless times with homeowners and businesses and was not limited to State Farm customers. State Farm, Allstate, Mississippi Farm Bureau, United Services Automobile Association, and Nationwide were the most prominent insurers in the Gulf Coast region, but they were not the only insurers to deny claims for this reason. Thousands of policyholders were surprised to discover that any Katrina claim that included damage caused by the combination of water and wind was subject to denial by their insurance carrier. When the wind and water issue appeared in relation to Katrina, a huge number of challenges arose to the clause's legality.

The Broussards decided to sue State Farm. They alleged that after Katrina, State Farm executives, faced with massive claims, created a novel wind-water "protocol" for their adjusters. It instructed the adjusters to deny a claim unless wind was the *sole independent* cause of the damage. This changed the way adjusters were to interpret the insurance policy, and, it was argued by attorneys for the claimants, changed the terms of the policy itself. State Farm and other insurers argued that their homeowners insurance policies covered damage from wind but not from water and that the policies excluded damage that could have been caused by a combination of both, even if hurricane-force winds preceded a storm's rising water.

In mid-January 2007, U.S. District Court Judge L. T. Senter, Jr. (of the Southern District of Mississippi, Southern Division–Gulfport) handed down the decision in the *Broussard v. State Farm* case.[4] Judge Senter ruled that State Farm could not prove that Katrina's storm surge was responsible for all of the damage to the Broussards' home, and he held that unless State Farm could prove what portion of the claim was due to flood and what portion was due to wind, the policyholder was entitled to payment for the wind damage.

The decision sent shock waves through the insurance community. In the ruling, the judge not only ordered the insurer to pay the full amount of the Broussards' claim ($223,292) for loss of their house, he also allowed the eight-person jury to assess punitive damages against State Farm. The jury awarded the Broussards $2.5 million for bad faith claims handling. In late January 2007, Judge Senter reduced that amount to $1 million. He also noted that the insurance company did not obtain any expert opinion on the Broussards' particular loss; instead, the company had established a blanket procedure called "the debris line"—in the event a home was reduced to a slab, all damages were unilaterally presumed by the insurance company to be caused by flood (not covered), thereby requiring the policyholder to bear the burden of proving the damages were caused by wind (covered).

The judge, in upholding the punitive damage entitlement for the Broussards, held that there was clear and convincing evidence "that Defendant acted in such a grossly negligent way as to evince willful, wanton, or reckless disregard for the rights of the Plaintiffs." State Farm requested a new trial, but on May 11, 2007, the request was denied. State Farm appealed Judge Senter's decision to the Fifth U.S. Circuit Court, which meant that the Broussards would not receive any money until the outcome of the appeal was determined. In May 2007, their attorney estimated that there would be no decision for a year or more. The Broussards had still not rebuilt their home.

Out of Outrage
A Move Toward Federal Regulation

Word of insurance claim denials in the wake of Katrina reverberated through the halls of Congress. Regulation of the insurance industry and the industry's policy writing and claims handling became a major subject of discussion. Criticism of the industry's procedures came from both the House of Representatives and the Senate, as well as from both sides of the aisle, Democratic and Republican.

In March 2006, Representative Gene Taylor (D, Mississippi) of Bay St. Louis, Mississippi—himself a homeowner whose insurance claim was denied (it has since been settled)—fired an initial shot across the bow of the insurance companies when he said, "There ought to be a national registry of child molesters and insurance company executives because I hold them in the same very low esteem." He accused the industry of conspiracy and "massive fraud." A State Farm representative, reacting to Taylor's claims, called them "absurd."

In March 2007, Taylor—now chair of the Congressional Hurricane Katrina Task Force—and Charlie Melancon (D, Louisiana), the task force vice chairman, released a report, "Katrina and Beyond: Recommendations for Legislative Action," which focused on proposed changes in the insurance industry. The report recommended federal oversight, the elimination of the federal antitrust exemption for the insurance industry provided for in the McCarran-Ferguson Act of 1945, and creation of a mandatory all-perils homeowners' policy. At the congressional hearing, Taylor testified before his own committee.[5]

Next, it was time for Senator Trent Lott (R, Mississippi) to take on the industry. Lott's home, on the shore in Pascagoula, Mississippi, was reduced to rubble by Katrina. (While in Alabama viewing Katrina damage on September 2, 2005, President George W. Bush promised to sit on the home's rebuilt porch.[6]) As it turned out, the senator too had been denied coverage, and he now set his sights on investigating insurance practices in the United States. Accusing insurers of insensitivity and outright meanness, Lott inserted a provision into legislation that Bush signed in October 2006, directing the Department of Homeland Security (DHS) to investigate potential fraud by the insurance industry.

As of late 2007, the DHS final report had not yet been issued. The interim report, released in August 2007 and based on a review of ninety-eight flood claims, did not uncover any fraud. However, the DHS did express concern over the carriers' potential conflict of interest, because insurers wrote both private property casualty homeowners (wind damage) insurance and policies under the National Flood Insurance Program (water damage), and then decided which claims should be submitted to the NFIP as flood claims. The DHS also expressed concern over insurers' policy language that excluded coverage if flooding occurred concurrently with wind or other causes of damage.[7]

Lott also drafted legislation to challenge the industry's exemptions from antitrust laws under the McCarran-Ferguson Act, and he asked his staff to investigate the industry's tax rates.[8] At this writing, the legislation had not yet been voted out of committee.

In October 2006, a little more than one year after Katrina, not only were many claims still outstanding, but charges had also surfaced of unethical claims-adjusting practices. CNN reported that trial attorney Richard "Dickey" Scruggs, representing a group of policyholders suing State Farm and other insurers, announced that he had evidence that damage reports had been altered to favor the insurance companies. In one case cited by Scruggs, although one engineering company twice told State Farm that wind was the predominant cause of the damage of the claimant's home (which would require the insurer to pay), State Farm commissioned a third opinion from another engineering firm, which found that the damage resulted from storm tide (the insurer would not have to pay). State Farm said it could not explain why the additional reports were ordered, since it was not the normal process.

On the heels of this allegation, Mississippi Attorney General Jim Hood commenced a state criminal investigation, and a grand jury was convened. Several witnesses appeared, including former employees of State Farm's adjusting company's subcontractor, who produced reams of internal claims records that they stated proved that the insurer defrauded policyholders by manipulating the engineering reports.[9] The investigation is ongoing.

Turning to the Courts

When Katrina policyholders started receiving claim denials, many turned to the state insurance regulators for help getting claims paid. The regulators tried, but they were largely unsuccessful. There was no unified central regulatory force leading the charge for the Gulf States claimants, and no uniform enforcement method to facilitate prompt and fair resolution of the claims. Once again, the federal government was precluded by the McCarran-Ferguson Act from enacting a uniform standard set of protections and enforcement methods. The claimants realized that there was no real incentive for the carriers to adjudicate or settle tough claims quickly. Thus, the claimants turned to the courts.

To fill the void, with the regulations not providing definition, the courts began doing so from the bench, and the claimants began winning. In August 2006, Judge Senter rejected Nationwide's attempts to cancel coverage for wind damage when the damage occurred in combination with the flood.[10] This was one of the first rulings on the Katrina claims by the judge. (Questions of interpretation of the policy, in accordance with state insurance law, are usually handled by the state courts. This case was heard in federal court because it involved a question of overall coverage.)

On November 29, 2006, U.S. District Court Judge Stanwood Duval (Eastern District of Louisiana–New Orleans) ruled that one must make a distinction between a "natural flood" and a "man-made flood." Judge Duval said the language in the insurance policies relating to flood coverage was ambiguous, and therefore unenforceable, insofar as how it applied to "man-made" flood disasters, such as those that may result from ruptures in negligently designed or maintained structures. The devastation resulting from the break in the levy caused by Katrina could be construed as man-made, and therefore the result of negligence for which the carrier would have to pay. Since the insurers provided the wording for the policies, the judge said he felt "constrained to interpret it against the insurers."[11]

Attorney General Hood filed suit on September 15, 2005, against five major insurance companies (State Farm, Allstate, Mississippi Farm Bureau, United Services Automobile Association, and Nationwide) for refusing to cover at least $2 billion in estimated damage from Katrina's storm surge. (State Farm's initial response was to accuse Hood of being politically motivated.) The insurance companies successfully moved the case to federal court, but on December 26, 2006, Judge Senter moved the case back to state court, in accordance with McCarran-Ferguson. Trials were scheduled to begin in state court in 2007 to determine how much damage to flooded homes and businesses resulted from high winds, and in January 2007, State Farm agreed to pay $50 million to 35,000 claimants. In June 2007, Hood filed to force State Farm to make the promised payment.[12]

Hundreds of other cases are pending, and if the decisions go against the carriers, the insurers have the right to appeal to a higher court. They have already announced their decision to appeal many of the decisions. Appeals take time, and when a claimant needs the insurance money to rebuild, time is on the side of the insurer. Since there is no uniform or expedited procedure to obtain funds for the policyholders, the insurance companies are in a position to settle claims at discounted values, sometimes for pennies on the dollar. In

November of 2007, the US Court of Appeals for the Fifth Circuit (Mississippi) in another case, affirmed the validity and enforceability of anti-current causation language and insurance policies under Mississippi law. The court stated that the language in a policy could be used to exclude water damage caused by Hurricane Katrina and that the clause was not ambiguous.[13] This issue will continue to cause heated debate.

Insurers at the Crossroads

In the wake of Katrina, insurers had a choice. They could take a hard-nosed stance and refuse to pay, thereby exposing themselves to greater scrutiny, or they could take the Lloyd's of London approach after the San Francisco earthquake and fire of 1906, when there was serious debate about whether the earthquake precluded coverage. Lloyd's decided to pay all its claims, disregarding the earthquake exclusion contained in its policies. That one act of paying the claims when the company could have opted to fight significantly boosted Lloyd's reputation as well as the reputation of the insurance industry.[14]

In 2007, almost one and a half years after the hurricane, certain large carriers, including State Farm—faced with a torrent of individual and class action lawsuits and bad press, which could have lasted years—opted to enter settlement negotiations with claimants en masse.

Katrina Claims
The Vulture Culture Made Visible

Katrina heightened public awareness of the financial devastation that can result from natural catastrophe if regulators do not make certain, in advance, that:

1. Insurance coverage and exclusions are clearly understood by the policyholder.
2. Ambiguous policy language is eliminated.
3. Swift adjudication processes are in place.
4. Strong enforcement tools are made available.
5. Protections and uniformity of laws are built into the system.

Katrina demonstrated that the current regulatory climate offers little satisfactory protection or resolution of claims at a time when claimants most need them. Many policyholders were left to lie on the beach as prey, exposed to the vagaries of misleading marketing, frustrated by policy ambiguity, weakened by a slow settlement and adjudicatory process, and, most of all forced out of desperation to settle for pennies on the dollar because of their poor bargaining position.

If one had to pick a single recent event that would act as a catalyst for the overhaul of the insurance industry, it would be August 2005's Hurricane Katrina. The monster natural disaster was a wake-up call to consumers, regulators, and insurers. The denial or underpayment of hundreds of thousands of Hurricane Katrina insurance claims received negative and widespread media attention and aroused the anger of the nation. The storm after Katrina still lives.

Notes

1. For an excellent article on the anti-concurrent causation clause, see Joseph B. Treaster, "Katrina: Small Clause Big Problem," *New York Times*, August 4, 2006, Business section, p. 1, http://www.nytimes.com/2006/08/04/business/ 04insure.html?pagewanted = 2. In the article, Jeffrey Kline Gilbert, an executive in charge of Katrina claims at Nationwide, was reported to have given this response of "read your policy" to a question under oath in a homeowner's lawsuit against Nationwide.
2. Ibid.
3. Risk Management Solutions (RMS), a Newark, California–based insurance

risk modeler, said on September 5, 2005, that it was boosting its projection for insured losses to between $40 billion and $60 billion, including $15 billion to $25 billion in claims related to the so-called "Great New Orleans Flood." RMS said its estimate for insured losses from flood damage was limited to private insurance coverage and did not include any anticipated federal flood insurance payments. It predicted that the total economic loss in the Gulf Coast region could be as much as $125 billion, http://rms.com/NewsPress/PR_090205_HUKatrina_insured_update.asp. See also, *Rick Jervis, USA Today*, August 28, 2007, "2 Years After Katrina: Pace of Rebuilding Depends on Who Pays," http://www.usatoday.com/news/nation/2007-08-28-rebuild_N.htm.

It was reported that none of the 115 "critical priority projects" identified by city officials has been completed: For example, New Orleans' police superintendent still works out of a trailer, as do most of the city's firefighters.

According to *USA Today*, the delays have affected the poor the most—those dependent on government assistance to rebuild their lives. While middle- and upper-class neighborhoods have rebuilt using private insurance and contacts, residents of low-income areas such as the Lower 9th Ward and Holy Cross—roughly 20,000 of them—for the most part remain scattered throughout the region, their return uncertain. . . . Of the $116 billion appropriated by Congress to Gulf Coast recovery, $34 billion has been earmarked for long-term rebuilding. But less than half of that has made its way through federal checks and balances to reach municipal projects.

In August 2007, the New Orleans' population, normally at about 300,000, was estimated at approximately 67 percent of what it was before Katrina. According to the Insurance Information Institute, the property/casualty insurance industry will pay out an estimated $40.6 billion on some 1.7 million claims in six states for Hurricane Katrina. By contrast, Hurricane Andrew, the previous record holder, resulted in $15.5 billion in losses in 1992 ($20.9 billion in today's dollars) and 790,000 claims, *Impact Magazine*, p. 1, http://www.iii.org/static/impactpdfs/impactwin05.pdf.

4. *Broussard v. State Farm Fire & Casualty Co.*, 1:06-cv-00006 LTS-RHW (USDC, Southern District of Mississippi, Southern Division–Gulfport), January 11, 2007.

5. Matt Brady, "Katrina Panel Hears Insurer Fraud Charges," National Underwriter Online News Service, March 1, 2007.

6. White House Press Release, September 2, 2005.

7. "Interim Report: No Proof Insurers Labeled Katrina Wind Claims as Flood," InsuranceJournal.com, August 16, 2007.

8. Joseph B. Treaster, "Insurers Get an Earful from Senator," *New York Times*,

October 12, 2006, Business/Financial Desk, p. 1, http://www.nytimes.com/2006/10/12/business/12insure.html.

9. Kathleen Koch, "CNN Presents: The Town that Fought Back," October 1, 2006. See also Michael Kunzelman, "Ex-State Farm Adjusters Tell Miss. Grand Jury of Katrina Claims," *Insurance Journal Online*, January 23, 2007, Southeast section.

10. *Leonard v. Nationwide Mutual*, 1:05 CV475 LTS-RHW (USDC, Southern District of Mississippi), August 16, 2006.

11. Joseph B. Treaster, "Judge Upholds Policyholders' Katrina Claims," *New York Times*, November 29, 2006, Business/Financial Desk, p. 2, http://www.nytimes.com/2006/11/29/business/29insure.html. See also "In Re Katrina Canal Breaches Consolidated Litigation," Civil Action number 05–4182, section "K"[2] (USDC, Eastern District of Louisiana).

12. Brian Kern, "State Farm Settles Miss. Katrina Lawsuits; Agrees to Reopen Other Miss. Claims," *Insurance Journal Online*, January 24, 2007.

13. Tuepker v. State Farm Fire and Casualty Co., United States Court of Appeals for the Fifth Circuit, App. No. 06-61075, November 6, 2007. The appellate court reaffirmed the holding in Leonard v. Nationwide Mutual Insurance Co., App. No. 06-61130, that flood exclusions in homeowner policies are valid under Mississippi law and can be used to exclude water damage caused by Hurricane Katrina. In Leonard, while allowing the anti-current causation language, the lower court created a shifting of burden of proof test (on wind verss water) between the plaintiff claimant and the defendant insurance company to determine whether the company had to pay; once the plaintiff presented evidence as to why the damage was caused by wind, the burden shifted to the defendant insurer to show why the plaintiff should not be paid.

14. Britton Wells, "Lloyd's Sees 1906 San Francisco Earthquake as a Turning Point," *Insurance Journal Online*, May 8, 2006, http://www.insurancejournal.com/magazines/west/2006/05/08/features/69899.htm.

International companies coming into the country.
Cartoon by Brad McMillan. Reprinted with permission of Cartoonstock.com.

CHAPTER 4

How the Industry Got Where It Is Today
Foreign Takeovers, Unregulated Reinsurers, Insurer and Claimant Fraud

"Management controls and risk analysis were abysmal. . . . [I]t will take years to sort out the mess."

—*Forbes*, January 10, 2000, discussing billion-dollar failure of offshore reinsurers operating with no federal and minimal state regulatory oversight

The Impact of Foreign Takeovers of U.S. Insurers

In the late 1990s and the early years of the 21st century, international takeovers of insurance companies took center stage. It was the era of alien (foreign) takeover of domestic insurers, and domestic insurers acquiring aliens. According to the National Association of Insurance Commissioners (NAIC), an "alien" insurer is an insurance company that is incorporated according to the requirements of a country other than the United States.[1] Under current law, the federal government cannot regulate insurance, so there is no federal body approving these new transactions, which leaves regulation of these acquisitions to the states.

Belgian, Dutch, French, and German powerhouse insurers bought up U.S. insurers and managed them, directly or indirectly, from outside the United States. For example, by the end of the 1990s, AEGON NV (a Dutch company) had bought Transamerica for $10.8 billion, Fortis (a Belgian company) had bought American Bankers Insurance for $2.62 billion, and ING (another Dutch company) had bought ReliaStar and bid on a portion of Aetna.

Credit Lyonnais, a French bank, together with a consortium of wealthy French nationals, attempted to buy Executive Life Insurance Company. However, the group violated U.S. law, since the Glass-Steagall Act prohibits ownership of any U.S. insurer by a foreign bank. The French government (which took over Credit Lyonnais) pleaded guilty in January 2004 in U.S. District Court in California to fraud, agreeing to pay the U.S. Treasury a $770 million fine—the biggest criminal settlement in U.S. history. Credit Lyonnais, the French government, and several wealthy French nationals (including billionaire François Pinault, who apparently garnered a $2.54 billion profit and was reportedly a close friend of French President Jacques Chirac) admitted that they had circumvented U.S. law and California state law, which also barred foreign bank ownership of U.S. insurers. Had the acquisition of the U.S. insurer been attempted by a French insurance company instead of a French bank consortium, it is likely that there would have been no violation of U.S. or state law because there are no federal insurance laws regulating acquisitions by a foreign insurer of a U.S. insurer.

Other companies from other countries evidenced a strong interest in acquiring U.S. insurance firms. For example, Ace Ltd. (Bermuda) bought CIGNA's property and casualty operations for $3.5 billion. Now that relations with China have been normalized, there no doubt could be international insurance deals involving China in the future.[2]

This flurry of acquisition activity occurred because insurance stocks were cheap and the insurance market fragmented. In addition, generally rising stock prices and low interest rates made financing takeovers easier, and some foreign buyers were attracted by the chance to own a dominant share of the U.S. marketplace.

The acquisitions slowed after the flurry of activity, in part because in 2000, the U.S. stock market bubble burst. In addition, since 2001, acquisition of U.S. insurers by foreign purchasers slowed as a result of weak economic conditions overseas.[3] Nevertheless, foreign insurers continued to be on the lookout for acquisition of U.S. insurers, and in June 2006, the acquisition train started to roll again. Swiss Re (Switzerland) announced that it had completed its acquisition of General Electric Insurance Solutions (GEIS) of Kansas City, Missouri, for $7.4 billion.[4] Swiss Re obtained approval of the merger from the European Commission and the state insurance commissioner. The transaction established Swiss Re as the world's largest life and health reinsurer and one of the world's leading reinsurers.

On the flip side, in the late 1990s, certain U.S. insurers announced that they were acquiring alien insurers. Liberty Mutual purchased segments of Guardian Royal Exchange PLC (a British subsidiary of Sun Life, owned by AXA, a French insurance group) for $1.5 billion. New York Life bought Kookmin Life (Korea), while Chubb acquired a license to sell insurance in China and acquired a substantial interest in Hiscox PLC (British).[5]

At present, foreign insurers acquiring U.S. assets are regulated only in the states in which they operate. International acquisitions have their place, if they make sense financially and if they provide the intended service. However, acquisitions also have to be regulated, so that the companies and executives are accountable to the U.S. government, as well as to the international marketplace, and to ensure proper oversight and enforceability of U.S. laws and regulations in this critical area. One state should not have the burden of acting on behalf of all the others, as is the case right now.

Unregulated Reinsurers
The Unspoken Problem

When customers purchase an insurance policy from a brand-name insurer, they may not know, understand, or care that a major portion of the risk may be "laid off" on another entity, known as a reinsurer. In industry parlance, a primary insurer is said to "lay off" or "cede" its risk to a reinsurer; in return, the primary insurer (the cedant) pays a premium to the reinsurer, which takes the bulk of the risk. Reinsurance is an important "sharing the risk" concept that enables an insured to get coverage that would normally be too great for any one insurance company to assume.

Reinsurance is a very big part of the insurance scene, and an even bigger potential problem. It is an aspect of insurance that has been largely ignored in terms of regulation. There is no uniform, formal audit/solvency test or federal regulatory agency responsible for the oversight of the reinsurers. This leaves a lot of monitoring responsibility up to an individual state, and nonuniform standards of oversight and reporting can become a major problem. Complicating matters in some cases is the fact that the reinsurer can transfer the risk even further to another reinsurer, known as a retrocessionaire.

Reinsurers can be domestic, out-of-state (called foreign insurers by the NAIC—incorporated in the United States, but operating outside the regulating state), or alien (domiciled outside the United States). The customer certainly will be unaware that a majority of reinsurers are from foreign countries (51.8 percent) and are not regulated by the U.S. government. "Offshore" reinsurers, in order of premium volume, are domiciled in Bermuda, Germany, Switzerland, the United Kingdom, the Cayman Islands, Barbados, Ireland, France, Turks and Caicos, Sweden, Japan, and Canada.[6]

If you add in the U.S. subsidiaries of alien reinsurers, the percentage of offshore reinsurers jumps to 84 percent.[7] For example, 2005's hurricane losses were borne as follows: 45 percent in the private insurer market, 23 percent among Bermuda reinsurers, 11 percent among U.S. reinsurers, 13 percent among European reinsurers, and 8 percent in Lloyd's (which operates out of London but has international constituents).[8]

Since the majority of reinsurers are foreign or alien, and therefore unregulated, failures of reinsurers can cause huge financial problems.[9] In 1999, for example, unregulated reinsurer broker Unicover (Bermuda) wrote billions of dollars of workers compensation reinsurance on behalf of blue-chip reinsurers that were eager to take risks that observers now believe lacked the potential for adequate returns. One of the problems, as reported in *Forbes*, was that "management controls and risk analysis were abysmal." In addition, several companies taking the reinsurance risk were life insurance specialists and "were not sophisticated . . . about pricing casualty contracts, and ended up taking in $700 million of premiums in return for a potential future payout of $2.8 billion."[10] According to the *Forbes* article, Unicover wrote far more reinsurance than the reinsurers had authorized, and no one knew who would pay the workers compensation claims.[11]

When Unicover failed in 1999 (to the tune of a $1.3 billion liquidation), major primary U.S. insurers were affected (including Reliance, which in 1999 took an after-tax charge of $100 million as a result of Unicover's failure, significantly compromising Reliance's financial status). Thereafter, a General Accounting Office study revealed significant problems with the oversight of the reinsurance industry, and a congressional inquiry was started about why, in the wake of Unicover, the states failed to adopt the NAIC's model regulations on reinsurance. (As of late 2007, there had been no answer to this question, nor had the states adopted any uniform regulation.)

In 2006, reinsurance specialists could not get a handle on the strength of the reinsurance market after Katrina as they reviewed whether the massive losses would sink the reinsurers, and consequently, cause the whole insurance package to collapse. One independent research specialist, noting that reinsurance covered 48 percent of the Katrina claims, said that "While the financial impact on casualty lines from the 2005 hurricanes is still unknown, the significant property losses prompted casualty cedants to reevaluate the financial position of their reinsurers."[12]

The experts believed that reinsurance capacity was still there, but they noted a number of serious problems. They said that the main industry rating agencies (Standard & Poor's, A.M. Best, and Fitch) were getting concerned. Rating downgrades outnumbered upgrades, and S&P lowered its outlook on the reinsurance sector from stable to negative. They reported that primary carriers were becoming "ever more security conscious" as to the financial stability of reinsurers.[13] There were no reports of reinsurer failures in 2007, but the reinsurance specialist report noted that, in 2006, the industry was still sorting out claims from natural disasters of 2002.[14] And who supervises the speculative investments? No one.[15]

Interestingly, a congressional committee headed by Representative John Dingell, Jr. (D, Michigan) predicted the problem of an unregulated reinsurance business almost twenty years ago when it observed that the insurance industry treats "the reinsurance process as a way to pass loss problems to somebody else in exchange for easy premium dollars, rather than as a prudent method to share risks."[16]

The state insurance commissioners are keenly aware of the reinsurer problem, but they seem powerless to do anything about it. In January 2002, they met to discuss imposing regulations on reinsurers. However, observers predicted that this would not likely develop into concrete proposals, in part, they said, because "it would face fierce opposition from U.S. reinsurers that must compete with companies overseas."[17] In 2007, a bill was introduced in Congress to regulate the reinsurers. However, until it or some other bill passes, the reinsurers remain virtually unregulated or, under the state system, under-regulated and nonuniformly regulated.

Holocaust Claims
The "Lost" Files and Other Cases

Toward the end of the 1990s, diligent investigators uncovered massive international insurance fraud perpetrated on victims of the Nazi Holocaust, and in 1999, the heirs of Holocaust victims began battling Assicurazioni Generali SpA, the giant Italian insurer, to recover millions in unpaid life insurance policies taken out by family members killed by the Nazis. The Italian insurance company at first said it had no legal liability for the claims, and then said it could not find the files.[18]

The company also set up rigid evidentiary rules for filing claims, including original papers that the heirs obviously would not have.

The California Insurance Department did not believe the Assicurazioni Generali response, so an official from the department was sent to Italy to look for the files. After months of searching through old warehouses in Trieste, the official finally found them. Confronted with the evidence, Assicurazioni Generali admitted liability.

The Assicurazioni case raised a legal problem: Should a state have the power, jurisdictional authority, or ability to act in an international arena on behalf of its citizens? This question was squarely raised in the case of *American Insurance Association v. Garamendi* (John Garamendi was at the time the California insurance commissioner), which was argued before the U.S. Supreme Court in April 2003. In this case, California's Holocaust Victim Insurance Relief Act was criticized before the Court by the U.S. Solicitor General's office, which contended that the state was trying to establish its own foreign policy. In July 2003, the Court agreed and struck down the California law. In an ironic twist, the Court ruled that a federal agency with power over these issues would have been a better body to handle this international insurance issue than a well-intentioned state Insurance Department. The only problem is that no federal agency has power over insurance issues because the McCarran-Ferguson Act required the states to regulate the "business of insurance."

Many state governments are now investigating and collecting the funds owed to Holocaust survivors. Class action lawsuits were brought in New York on behalf of the heirs against several foreign insurance companies, including Allianz, Germany's giant insurer,[19] and ING, the Dutch financial and insurance services group that in 2000 was trying to acquire U.S. life insurer ReliaStar. Since ReliaStar was domiciled in Minnesota, the state of Minnesota had to undertake the task of reviewing these Holocaust issues when it reviewed ING's intended takeover of ReliaStar.[20]

While there is no question that Minnesota and California proceeded responsibly, as have some of the other states, the real question is why was the federal government not involved in this major international insurance issue?

Commendably, an international committee pressured the insurers to establish a fund for disbursement to the heirs, and on February 17, 1999, Chancellor Gerhard Schroeder of Germany announced that a fund projected to amount to $1.7 billion would be created and financed by twelve German companies (including Allianz) to compensate victims of the Nazis. The NAIC formed a multistate committee to administer the Holocaust insurance funds, and progress has been made to return the money to the heirs; however, as of late 2007, large portions of the funds ($300 million) still had not been distributed.

Insurer Fraud in the United States

While most insurers and claimants do not engage in fraud, those that do are rarely caught, and if they are, they rarely receive significant punishment. Let's look at some notable cases of insurer fraud.

In 1999, State Farm Insurance Company (whose slogan is "Like a Good Neighbor, State Farm Is There") had to pay a number of large-scale damage awards based on allegations of fraud, involving retirement investments and improper employee practices. In a settlement in an Illinois case, for example, State Farm agreed to pay $238 million in a class action suit that claimed fraudulent practices in selling life insurance. The jury found that State Farm had encouraged policyholders to switch policies, thereby losing value on the original policy, and further that the company had sold life insurance as "investment" and "retirement" plans, which, the jury believed, they clearly were not.

In 1999, an Alaska jury required State Farm to pay $153 million in punitive damages to a former agent who was fired for refusing to market life insurance products as "good investments," when the rate of return was lower than that of stocks, bonds, and other investments. The agent, instead of pitching State Farm's brochures, advised his customers (against the orders of State Farm) to buy other investments. State Farm threatened to appeal and, although it was unlikely that the higher court would reverse the decision (according to observers), the case was settled with the agent for $7.5 million.

In another case, in 1998, State Farm paid more than $100 million to settle a lawsuit alleging it covertly trimmed earthquake policies in California.[21]

In October 1999, in a case involving auto insurance policies, an Illinois court ordered the insurer to pay $1.2 billion for instructing all repair shops to use generic replacement ("after-market") parts, without advising the policyholders. The scheme raised safety concerns while allowing State Farm to save millions of dollars on its claims. After the award, State Farm promised to correct the situation.[22]

Other U.S. insurance firms have also been accused of fraud. In the mid-1990s, Prudential Insurance Co. ("The Rock"), headquartered in Newark, New Jersey, had to pay fines and damages in excess of $600 million for fraudulent sales practices in both its securities and insurance units. In 1993, Prudential Securities established a $330 million settlement fund and paid $41 million in fines for fraudulently selling oil and gas partnerships as safe investments and misleading investors about the rates of return on the partnership. In 1994, Prudential doubled the settlement fund with another $330 million and settled lawsuits alleging insurance agent fraud following a $25.4 million jury award.[23]

Allstate ("You're in Good Hands with Allstate") has also been charged. In 1998, in an attempt not to pay or to severely limit the amount of payment for serious structural damage arising from an earthquake in Northridge, California, on January 17, 1994—a quake that caused approximately $25 billion in damages—Allstate was alleged to have hired unlicensed and questionable experts, falsified documents with counterfeit engineering stamps, and "squeaked the file." An Allstate official admitted that the company's claims handling "was an unfortunate mistake," and Allstate reopened thousands of claims. According to ABC-TV, the fraud was alleged to involve tens of millions of dollars. The allegations led to a federal grand jury investigation of Allstate and the firm's corporate headquarters being raided by FBI agents looking for incriminating documents.[24] It led to the conviction in 2004 of an independent claims adjuster hired by Allstate (seven years in prison), as well as the conviction in 2002 of an engineering expert, who was sentenced to eighty-seven months in prison and ordered to pay $1.17 million in restitution.

In 2002, fraud was revealed in the MEWA (Multiple Employer Welfare Arrangement) arena. MEWAs act on behalf of small unions or businesses that band together in special group arrangements to insure their members or employees, usually for health insurance. MEWAs were largely unregulated healthcare buying groups, with virtually no oversight by state insurance departments.

Although in 1983, Congress amended the Employee Retirement Income Security Act of 1974 (ERISA) preemption provision to permit states to regulate MEWAs, state laws vary, and some states do not even regulate all MEWAs. As a result, the 3 million or so Americans covered by this vehicle had no one protecting their interests. Self-insured plans established or maintained by a union or a single employer remain exempt from most state insurance regulation.

Most MEWAs folded, and many doctors performing medical services for MEWA policyholders went unpaid. Employers Mutual, a small MEWA, took in approximately $14 million in premiums, paid out $3 million in claims, and is now out of business. No one knows where the rest of the Employers Mutual money is.[25]

In some states, even the regulators have been convicted of fraud. In Louisiana, state Insurance Commissioner Jim Brown was indicted for conspiracy, witness tampering, and mail fraud. This followed two other former Louisiana insurance commissioners who were convicted and sent to federal prison (Sherman Bernard for taking bribes and Doug Green for violation of campaign disclosure laws, including hiding the fact that his $2 million election campaign was funded by an auto insurer that later collapsed as a result of fraud). In April 2000, four-time Louisiana Governor Edwin Edwards was convicted in federal court on a multi-count indictment, stemming from his plot to block the state's efforts to recoup money from the owner of a failed insurance company. In Tennessee (as discussed in Chapter 3), the insurance commissioner resigned amid the collapse of Martin Frankel's Thunor Trust insurance group and the Frankel insurance fraud and embezzlement scandal.[26]

Fraud by Individual and Business Claimants

On the other side of the ledger are the millions of dollars stolen from insurers each year by individuals and businesses using improper and fraudulent means. The Coalition Against Insurance Fraud, a broad-based nonprofit organization founded in 1993 to combat individual claimant insurance fraud, estimates that individual claimant fraud costs U.S. businesses $80 billion per year. The coalition's board of directors includes insurance carriers, consumer groups, state police, civic organizations, and others, and its mission is to alert the public about individual and business claimant fraud.[27]

In the United States, insurance fraud is estimated to cost $875 per year for every person in the country. Medicare officials estimate false insurance claims in the US healthcare system at $179 billion per year.[28] Despite this large amount, there is no public clamor about individual claim fraud, so the issue has not become a high-profile news story or generated highly prosecuted civil or criminal offenses.

Since insurance fraud is not a crime of violence, prosecutors and the media sometimes look on it as a "Robin Hood" event, where the claimant is robbing from the rich (the all-powerful insurance carrier) and giving to the poor (the downtrodden claimant). As a result, some prosecutors and some in the media are less apt to go after or report on cases of claimant insurance fraud.

To their credit, states are beginning to notify fraudulent insurance claimants of the government's intolerance of such actions. New Jersey, for example, has run television and radio advertising campaigns warning offenders about the serious consequences of insurance fraud and the possibility of jail time.

In 1994, Pennsylvania's legislature created the Pennsylvania Insurance Fraud Prevention Authority (IFPA), which supports the investigation and prosecution of individuals who commit insurance fraud. It also acts to educate citizens about the crime of insurance fraud. All insurers doing business in Pennsylvania are assessed a sum of money for fraud prevention based on the number of policies written in the state. The IFPA obtained funds for television, radio, websites, billboards, and press releases to warn individuals against insurance fraud, as well as for investigative purposes.

New York has become active in the auto insurance area, since the prevalence of automobile insurance fraud in New York is a significant contributor to high automobile insurance rates in the state. On May 9, 2001, Governor George Pataki signed Executive Order 109, which designated the attorney general as special prosecutor to coordinate the investigatory and prosecutorial efforts related to fraudulent auto insurance claims. An Auto Insurance Fraud Unit was set up in the attorney general's office. As of 2005, the Auto Insurance Fraud Unit had brought felony insurance fraud and related charges against 272 defendants. Also in 2005, the attorney general's office announced a seventy-two–count indictment against eight suspects and one law firm allegedly involved in submitting fraudulent no-fault and bodily injury claims to insurance carriers. These indictments sought the forfeiture of $2.2 million in illegally obtained proceeds. Auto insurance fraud in New York is estimated by the attorney general's office at $1 billion per year.[29]

The actions of the New York Auto Insurance Fraud Unit have had a definite impact on the marketplace. Since 2002, there has been a significant decline in losses for private passenger automobile insurance, and the New York Insurance Department called on insurers to reduce their rates. To date, the Insurance Department has approved a record number of auto rate reductions, saving policyholders almost $400 million per year. More than twenty auto insurers—including the top three in terms of market share, Allstate, GEICO, and State Farm—reduced their rates an average of 5 percent in 2005.[30]

The Insurance Information Institute reported in July 2007 that, as of 2005, there were forty states with fraud bureaus; however, some had limited powers, and some addressed fraud in other types of businesses. The III also noted a study conducted by the Coalition Against Insurance Fraud, covering the period 2001–2006, which reported that the number of tips about suspected claimant fraud, cases opened and presented for prosecution, convictions, and restitution ordered increased by 20 percent during 2004–2005. Since then, the average number of prosecutions has been flat, and convictions have been down at many of the fraud bureaus. However, the study reported that in some states and localities, auto insurance premiums dropped between 11 percent and 24 percent, and the incidence of claimant fraud has declined since word of the fraud bureaus has spread.[31]

Insurance fraud means that money, which could otherwise be used for proper insurance purposes, is lost. Moreover, that money is ultimately paid for by all insurance customers through increased premiums, additional state taxes, and/or decreased benefits. Insurance fraud should be treated as a serious crime.

Notes

1. NAIC, *Insurance Department Resources Report 2002* (NAIC, 2003), p. 30.
2. These transactions and others involving insurance companies were regularly

reported in the U.S. press. For Ace Ltd., see *Philadelphia Inquirer*, February 20, 1999. For AEGON NV, see *Wall Street Journal*, March 12, 1999; *Philadelphia Inquirer*, February 20, 1999; and Bloomberg News, February 18, 1999. For Allianz AG, see Bloomberg News, February 6, 1999. For Fortis, see *New York Times*, February 1, 1999. For the French involvement in Executive Life, see John Carreyou and Glenn R. Simpson, "How Insurance Spat Further Frayed U.S.-French Ties," *Wall Street Journal*, April 16, 2004.

3. *New York Times*, March 9, 1999; see also Bureau of Economic Analysis, U.S. Department of Commerce, June 3, 2003.

4. "Swiss Re, GE Insurance Solutions Wrap Up Sale," *Kansas City Business Journal*, June 12, 2006, http://kansascity.bizjournals.com/kansascity/stories/2006/06/12/daily7.html?jst = m_ln_hl&surround = lfn.

5. Over the years, newspapers were full of stories about U.S. insurers seeking to acquire alien insurers. For Liberty Mutual, see *New York Times*, February 1, 1999; for New York Life, see Bloomberg News, March 31, 1999; for Chubb, see Bloomberg News, March 31, 1999.

6. Robert P. Hartwig, President, Insurance Information Institute, "Why 2008 is Shaping Up to Be a Make or Break Year for the P/C Insurance Industry," PowerPoint presentation to State Insurance Trade Association annual meeting, Seattle, Washington, September 25, 2007, slides 120 and 121; citing as source Insurance Information Institute and Reinsurance Association Of America. At present, the top 10 domiciles for "offshore." alien reinsurers who are unaffiliated with any United States re-insurer are located in (in descending order) Turks and Caicos (538 companies), Bermuda (412), United Kingdom (295), Cayman Islands (176), Island of Nevis (128), British Virgin Islands (55), Barbados (48), Belgium (48), Germany (45), and Ireland (45). Additionally, the alien reinsurer market share is growing (less than 40% in 1997 compared to 53% in 2006), and the US reinsurer market share is correspondingly shrinking.

7. Ibid.

8. Ibid

9. Robert Lenzner and Bernard Condon, "Passing the Trash," *Forbes*, January 10, 2000, p. 60.

10. Ibid.

11. Ibid.

12. "Swings and Roundabouts: Reinsurance Market and Renewals Review," Benfield Ltd., January 2006.

13. Ibid.

14. Ibid.

15. Pammy Olson, "Swiss Re Tanks on Subprime Loss" see Forbes.com, November 19, 2007 Swiss Re, the world's biggest reinsurer, created havoc for its company in November 2007 (an unexpected payout of $900 million to one of its insureds, causing a one-day drop in stock price of 10.3%) based on aggressive underwriting decisions it had made to insure the investor's portfolio values in the subprime mortgage market. Swiss Re refused to reveal the name of its policyholder receiving this money. Once this payment was revealed, analysts and investors started to worry as to how isolated this type of transaction is in the reinsurance market. The news raised the question: what would happen if these unregulated reinsurers made a series of aggressive, improper underwriting decisions, causing the reinsurers to suffer such losses that they may be unable to pay the claims of other unsuspecting policyholders? What government entity is protecting the rest of the policyholders, who expected solvency and prudent management?

16. Ibid.

17. "Failed Promises," 1990 House Committee Report. Report by the Subcommittee on Oversight and Investigation of the Committee on Energy and Commerce, *Failed Promises, Insurance Company Insolvencies*, U.S. House of Representatives 101st Congress, 2nd Session 2 (1990) (also known as *Dingell Report*).

18. Ibid. Also see David Cay Johnston, *New York Times*, August 20, 1998 . . . "Italian Insurer Agrees to Pay 100 Million in Holocaust Suit," Section A, p. 8, col. 5, Foreign Desk; Roger Cohen, "Chancellor Announces Fund for Victims of Nazis," *New York Times*, February 17, 1999 . . . "German Companies Adopt Fund for Slave Laborers Under Nazis," Section A, p. 1, col. 1, Foreign Desk; Robert Greenberger, "The Patriarch's Insurance Policies: Holocaust Victim Foresaw Horror, but Insurer Balks," *Wall Street Journal*, March 26, 1999, p. B1.

19. Johnston, *New York Times*, August 20, 1998; Roger Cohen, "Chancellor Announces Fund for Victims of Nazis," *New York Times*, February 17, 1999.

20. "ING buys U.S. insurer ReliaStar for $6.1 bln," Reuters, May 1, 2000; see also Joan Gralla, "World, Dutch Jews Weigh Boycott Against Stock Market," Reuters, May 22, 2000.

21. Associated Press, February 12, 1999; see also Insurance News Network, March 8, 1999, and *Bellott v. State Farm* (Alaska Superior Court, Third Judicial District), jury verdict, March 3, 1999.

22. *Philadelphia Inquirer*, October 9, 1999, p. 1.

23. *Best's Review, Life-Health Insurance Edition*, December 1994.

24. Brian Ross, "Allegations Against Allstate After L.A. Quake—Transcript of 'A Policy For Profit?'" *20/20*, ABC-TV, October 14, 1998.

25. Judy Muller, "World News Tonight with Peter Jennings," ABC-TV, March 6, 2002.

26. "Judge Reaches Plea Agreement, Will Testify against Commissioner," *Business Insurance*, October 11, 1999; see also Scott J. Paltrow, "Bad Policies? Down in Louisiana Insurance Regulation Carries a Strange Risk; Two Commissioners Went to Prison, the Latest Finds Himself Indicted; Clues in a Roguish History," *Wall Street Journal*, November 19, 1999.

27. See www.insurancefraud.org.

28. "Insurance Fraud," expertwitness.com, available at http://www.expertwitness.com/lbct/2783/insurance-fraud.htm.

29. Press Release, New York State Attorney General's Office, 2005.

30. New York State Attorney General's Office, 2005.

31. "Insurance Fraud," Issue Updates position paper, Insurance Information Institute, July 2007.

Jumping through hoops to get insurance coverage.
Cartoon by Brian Duffy, *The Des Moines Register*. Reprinted with permission of the artist.

CHAPTER 5

The View from Outside
A Report Card on State Regulation

"[M]uch work remains to be done". . . . "spotty coverage". . . .
"inconsistent". . . . "potential gaps in consumer protection". . . . "no
generally accepted standards exist for market conduct regulation."
    —General Accounting Office, "Common Standards and Improved
      Coordination Needed to Strengthen Market Regulation," September 2003

A Report Card from the Consumer Federation of America

J. Robert Hunter, director of insurance of the Consumer Federation of America (CFA), greeted me at the National Press Club in downtown Washington, D.C., on a cold Wednesday morning in March 1999. The CFA is a national network of approximately 300 proconsumer groups, a watchdog organization representing more than 50 million people. Its mission is to advance the consumer interest through advocacy and education. Hunter—who is called Bob—is specifically well versed in the requirements and standards for running a proper insurance commissioner's office, having been insurance commissioner for the state of Texas, one of the largest states in insurance premium volume. He also served as federal insurance administrator, in charge of the federal flood insurance program, in the Ford and Carter administrations.

At the Press Club, Hunter presented the CFA's first report card on the states to a packed audience. The report, titled "Consumer Information Available from State Insurance Departments," presented the results of a three-month study on how well the state insurance departments make information available to the consumer in written form (such as brochures). The grades were not good.

The CFA gave only seven states out of fifty an A rating. Most states (twenty-six) fell in the middle, with Bs or Cs. A surprising seventeen states—more than a third—received a D, F, or I (incomplete, which meant the state didn't even respond). One state had no written material whatsoever for the consumer.[1] The CFA concluded that while a few states were doing a job worthy of an A, others needed to substantially upgrade their services to help consumers knowledgeably shop for and choose among insurance products. Hunter then explained how this lack of information harmed the consumer, and he criticized most of the states for not having consumer-friendly information, such as brochures in easy-to-understand language and comparative price information and information about the financial stability of the various carriers.

While the CFA study was immediately criticized by the National Association of Insurance Commissioners (NAIC) as being too subjective, it received wide media exposure, especially in those states receiving a failing grade.

During the end of the 1990s and the early years of this decade, the CFA produced several other studies regarding the way states protect the consumer. The CFA's follow-up study, "Insurance Department Grades for Consumer Complaint Information" (May 1999), surveyed the availability and usefulness of information that states make available to consumers on the quality of insurance as measured by complaint ratios, in which it compared the level of consumer dissatisfaction with competing insurance companies. In that report, the CFA suggested ways insurance departments could better communicate with consumers.[2]

In a third study on consumer information, "Internet Webpage Grades," which was completed in 2002, the CFA reviewed each state's website for the availability of information about price competition and complaint filing online. The results were better. CFA reported that over one-half of the population lives in states with excellent webpage information (15 states)[3] CFA has not yet produced any update on studies of consumer information available through state insurance departments.

Another important study by the CFA, "Minimum Funding Standards," released in 2000, concluded that about 75 percent of Americans live in states whose insurance departments do not meet the CFA's minimum funding standards for properly overseeing the insurance industry in their respective states. The CFA defines "minimum standard" as a state insurance department budget that is at least equal to 10 percent of the tax revenues collected by the state from insurance premiums paid by state policyholders. Most state insurance departments receive well below 10 percent of the insurance premium tax revenue. The rest of the money goes to other state projects.[4]

The average funding for the state insurance departments nationwide as a percentage of insurance premium tax revenue collected was 7.99 percent in 2000—20 percent lower than the funding CFA believed it should be. In 2006, the average funding for the state insurance departments nationwide as a percentage of insurance premium tax revenue collected was 7.11 percent—30 percent lower than the 10 percent the CFA believed it should be. These numbers are important because they reflect the attitude held by many legislators that the insurance department budgets were good enough.

Although Hunter has been openly critical of the insurance industry in many areas, he is well respected as an actuary and a knowledgeable, experienced straight shooter. Hunter and the CFA staff have testified numerous times before Congress and have written well-researched position papers on many insurance issues.[5] The CFA is an important force in shaping the debate and creating a voice for insurance consumers. Thus, when Bob Hunter and the CFA say the state-regulated insurance system disregards the consumer, has broken down, and needs to be fixed, as they have many times and continue to say, we should listen.

A Report Card from the GAO

In October 1979, the federal government took a major in-depth look at the effectiveness and impact of state regulation of the insurance industry when the General Accounting Office (GAO)—the watch-dog arm of Congress—studied the industry. (In 2004, the GAO's name was changed to the Government Accountability Office.) In 2003, the GAO did another study of the industry and found that the problems still exist.

The 1979 report was titled "Issues and Needed Improvements in State Regulation of the Insurance Business." The GAO was very critical of the way states regulated the industry, especially the lack of specific standards among the states. The GAO noted the need for:

- More experience and better salaries for regulators

- An "early warning system" to detect insurers' potential financial problems

- Analysis of consumer complaints

- Explicit uniform standards to evaluate companies, to be used in market conduct examinations

- A requirement that states examine and monitor claims handling performance

- More consumer information on such things as competitor pricing

- The elimination of redlining (discrimination based on geographic location)

- Centralized standards, such as policy language, data analysis, and uniform laws, which would result in economies of scale

- An arms-length relationship between the regulators and the regulated (the report indicated that regulators were overly responsive to the needs of the insurance industry at the expense of consumers)

- A standardized procedure for reviewing claims payment and rate setting, and for protecting consumers from discrimination[6]

It is interesting to note that in 1979, the GAO said something surprisingly similar to the situation that exists today:

> While critics of state regulation may overstate the extent of the "revolving door" problem, about half of the state insurance commissioners were previously employed by the insurance industry and roughly the same proportion joined the industry after leaving office, and NAIC meetings are numerically dominated by insurance industry representatives. Its model laws and regulations were drafted with advisory committees composed entirely of insurance company representatives.[7]

The GAO continues to monitor the industry with periodic reports to Congress on specific topics. On June 18, 2002, the GAO reported that "ongoing federal oversight and possibly federal intervention . . . may be needed to provide impetus for positive change and continuing improvements in state regulation of insurance."[8]

In September 2003, the GAO released a new study of the industry's market regulation, entitled "Common Standards and Improved Coordination Needed to Strengthen Market Regulation." Not surprisingly, the GAO identified the same major problems that existed in 1979. It included all the problems under the need for "market regulation," which the GAO defined as "the set of regulatory processes and tools focused on an insurance company's interactions with its customers." The GAO concluded that it is uncertain whether the states are capable of implementing the standardization of market conduct regulation. The GAO reiterated "the need for the states to improve the quality and uniformity of insurance regulation."[9]

The GAO continued its sweeping criticism of the regulatory system and urged a "common set of standards for a uniform market oversight program." The report stated:

> NAIC has been pursuing initiatives since the 1970s to improve uniformity in standards and procedures for a market analysis program and market conduct examinations, but progress has been

limited. . . . Recently, NAIC set as one of its major goals improving the way states use market analysis and market conduct examinations. However, it remains uncertain whether NAIC and the states can agree on and implement a program that will result in the standardization of market conduct regulation. Much work remains to be done to promote the coordination and cooperation that are needed for consistent market conduct regulation to protect insurance consumers.[10]

The 2003 GAO report repeatedly used words and phrases such as "much work remains to be done," "spotty coverage," "inconsistent," and "potential gaps in consumer protection." It concluded that "no generally accepted standards exist for market conduct regulation" to describe NAIC and state efforts toward uniformity. Among its conclusions were the following:

- States vary in how they conduct and how often they use market analysis and market conduct examinations.

- Market analysis and examinations need significant improvement.

- The NAIC has long recognized the need to improve market regulation but has made slow progress with its initiatives.[11]

Market conduct regulation—for example, oversight of insurance company practices such as selling and underwriting policies—needs to be given high priority, as does over-seeing insurance companies' financial solvency.

The 2003 report thus concluded that market regulation is based on overlapping and often inconsistent state policies and activities. The GAO observed that while the state insurance regulatory system provides some oversight, it may also place an undue burden on some insurance companies, and, at times, may fail to adequately protect consumers. It recommended:

. . . that NAIC and the states give increased priority to identifying a common set of standards for a uniform market oversight program that includes all states. These standards should include procedures for conducting market analysis and coordinating market conduct examinations. Further, NAIC needs to establish a mechanism to encourage state legislatures and insurance departments to adopt and implement the standards.[12]

Unfortunately, as of the end of 2007, uniform generally accepted standards for market conduct regulation do not exist among the states. Since the GAO has concluded that significant improvement will likely be slow in coming in the current state insurance regulatory environment, and since pressure is building for reform on the federal level, Congress may finally be ready to take matters into its own hands.

A Report Card from the NAIC

The NAIC, the insurance industry's self-regulating association, offers its own report card on the states in its annual publication, "Insurance Department Resources Report." The latest report published in 2007 with 2006 figures is chock-full of information and also includes some disturbing facts. Among them are the following:

■ A very large number of formal written consumer complaints are filed each year with the state insurance departments: approximately 400,000 per year, or more than 33,000 formal complaints per month; this is an average of more than 7,600 formal complaints per week. The level of complaints for the past five years has remained approximately the same. In addition, the NAIC reports that the state insurance departments received more than 2.5 million inquiries annually. The NAIC keeps no record of how these complaints or inquiries are resolved.

- Only a small percentage of revenue collected by the states' premium tax actually goes to support the state insurance department. An average of only 7.11 percent of the total revenue collected from insurance companies goes to insurance department operations.

- Most states do not have a dedicated consumer advocate's office on their insurance roster; in fact, only 20 out of 50 states (40 percent) have a consumer advocate's office at all. This leaves a whopping 60 percent of states that have no such office. There has been no increase in the number of consumer advocate offices in the past five years.

- Only the domiciliary state is responsible for auditing a particular insurance company, and each state relies heavily on the quality and efficiency of its fellow state regulators. In some states, these audits take place only once every three to five years.

- The report says nothing about control over the reinsurers, nor does it contain any information about reinsurance, over which the NAIC has no control.[13]

The fifty state insurance commissioners are members of the NAIC, as are the insurance commissioners from Washington, D.C. and the four territories (American Samoa, Guam, Puerto Rico, and U.S. Virgin Islands). The NAIC holds quarterly meetings that are attended by the commissioners, regulators, state insurance department staff, and other interested parties.

Insurance regulators in each state vary considerably in approach, experience, and attitude. Industry observer Andrew Tobias highlighted this problem in *The Invisible Bankers*, when he observed that insurers really act as bankers charged with properly investing and safeguarding the policy holders' money and the regulators have to be watchdogs. He also stated that "regulators vary markedly in the degree to which they are overwhelmed by the task at hand. Some are completely overwhelmed but seem not to care. Others are completely overwhelmed but try hard anyway."[14] Although the book was published more than twenty years ago, Tobias's observation is still valid today.

The recommendations of the NAIC to its state insurance commissioners, while attempting to tackle the hard questions of the industry, are merely that: recommendations, not hard and fast rules or binding laws. The NAIC is a voluntary body and has no statutory or enforcement powers of its own. Nevertheless, it is still a useful organization. It produces meaningful statistics and well-documented topical discussions and serves as an important monitoring and advisory system for all of the states.

For the last ten years, NAIC statistics demonstrate serious problems in the industry, which, for the most part, seem to emanate from the differences in state budgets, tax structures, administrative staffing, and enforcement. For example, insofar as monitoring the solvency of insurance companies is concerned, every NAIC State Insurance Department Resources Report reveals that each state's insurance regulators focus primarily on those insurance companies that are domiciled (incorporated) in that state. Monitoring of companies not domiciled in that state is left to regulators in the domiciliary state. The NAIC report acknowledges, almost warns, that the domicile system of monitoring results in each state placing heavy reliance on the quality and efficiency of its fellow state regulators.[15]

The NAIC also notes that while all states may supply information to it about the number of consumer complaints filed with the various state commissioners, the NAIC has no information about how many consumer claims were resolved to the satisfaction of the consumer, or even how many consumer claims were resolved at all.

Thus, based on the industry's own assessment, it seems reasonable to conclude that the insurance consumer is grossly underrepresented and that changes to the system are needed.[16]

The NAIC has been keenly aware for years of the issue of federal versus state insurance regulation. Rather than being an adversary to a federal system, the NAIC, with some creativity, could play a vital role in assisting in the restructuring of the insurance regulatory system as well as in the enforcement of the new system. It has the experience, infrastructure, and personnel to handle those assignments. It will, however, take key leadership to change the NAIC's current orientation from state regulation to a federal regulatory program.

The Industry Leaders
Setting Standards and Evaluating Job Performance

The need for accurate statistics and analysis is obvious. The NAIC strives to maintain accuracy and to compile the statistics on a consistent basis. However, the NAIC is the first to admit that because of differences among state insurance departments, this is not always possible. A look at job performance information published by individual states demonstrates that, in some cases, state insurance departments actually disseminate ineffective and misleading information.

For example, in a press release issued several years ago, Diane Koken, Pennsylvania's insurance commissioner, announced that "Last year [1998] our Consumer Services Bureau responded to approximately 20,000 written complaints and recovered more than $6 million for consumers."[17] On the surface, that seems fairly good work and it makes the department appear quite effective. On further investigation, though, a different picture emerged.

In March 2000, I interviewed the head of the Consumer Services Bureau of the Pennsylvania Insurance Department. The spokesperson explained that they used the phrase "responded to complaints" quite broadly. For example, sending the most perfunctory first letter from the department to an insurance company and forwarding a copy of a complaint to an insurance company for comment counted as responses.[18]

I asked how many of the 20,000 written complaints filed in Pennsylvania in 1998 were actually resolved in favor of the complainant, or if they were resolved at all. The response was that the department's internal disposition records are not made public.[19] When I asked how many consumers actually benefited from the $6 million the state collected, in what amount, and what type of claim was pursued, the response was the same. In my opinion, the stories would be similar in many states.[20] Clearly, if inaccurate information is being disseminated, it is misleading; if it is interpreted incorrectly, the information will not be reliable.

The CFA, the GAO, and the NAIC have demonstrated serious weaknesses in the present system. All have issued report cards, and the grades were not very good. It is vital that we do better.

Notes

1. The grades were as follows: An A was received by Colorado, Florida, Kansas, Missouri, Ohio, Texas, and Wisconsin. B, C, or D was received by Alaska B+, Arizona C+, California B+, Connecticut B−, Delaware C+, Hawaii C, Illinois B+, Indiana C+, Iowa B−, Kentucky C+, Louisiana C, Maine B, Massachusetts D, Michigan C+, Mississippi D+, Montana C−, Nebraska C+, Nevada B+, New Jersey D−, New Mexico D, New York B, North Carolina D+, North Dakota D+, Oklahoma C−, Oregon B−, Pennsylvania B−, South Carolina B−, Utah C, Vermont C−, Virginia B, Washington C+, West Virginia D+, and Wyoming C. An F was received by Georgia, Idaho, Rhode Island, South Dakota, and Tennessee. An I was received by Alabama, Arkansas, Maryland, Minnesota, and New Hampshire, as well as the District of Columbia. Regarding the incomplete grades, the CFA stated, "These are the

worst because we expect the inaction to a request by a major consumer group indicates that the typical consumer will be frustrated when approaching these states," http://www.consumerfed.org/topics.cfm?section = Finance&Topic = Insurance&SubT opic = Regulation.

2. NAIC's letter to CFA dated March 1999. The letter was shown to the author by CFA's Director of Insurance Robert Hunter on the day of CFA's presentation.

3. Consumer Federation of America, "Internet Webpage Grades," accessible at www.consumerfed.org, "Insurance."

4. *New York Times*, September 1, 2000; see also "Minimum Funding Standards," Consumer Federation of America, September 2000. The only states meeting the CFA's minimum funding standard in 2000 were Florida, Louisiana, Maine, Massachusetts, New York, Oregon, and Wyoming, as well as the District of Columbia, representing 17 percent of the population; and Alaska, Delaware, Illinois, Nebraska, New Jersey, and Vermont, as well as the U.S. Virgin Islands, representing 9 percent of the population.

5. See www.consumerfed.org, "Insurance," for an extensive list of articles.

6. Comptroller General of the United States, General Accounting Office Report to Congress, "Issues and Needed Improvements in State Regulation of the Insurance Business," October 9, 1979.

7. Comptroller General, "Issues and Needed Improvements."

8. "State Insurance Regulation," statement for the record by Richard J. Hillman, Director, Financial Markets and Community Investment, GAO Before the Subcommittee on Capital Markets, Insurance and Government Sponsored Enterprises, Committee on Financial Services, House of Representatives, June 18, 2002, www.gao.gov/cgi-bin/getrpt?GAO-02–842T.

9. Richard J. Hillman, "Common Standards and Improved Coordination Needed to Strengthen Market Regulation," Report to the Chairman, House Committee on Financial Services, General Accounting Office, Report GAO-03–433, Insurance Regulation, September 2003. See also the testimony of Morton A. Myers before the House Subcommittee on General Oversight and Minority Enterprise, Committee on Small Business, "Issues and Needed Improvements in State Regulation of the Insurance Business," October 22, 1979. Myers was deputy director of the Program Analysis Division of the GAO.

10. Hillman, "Common Standards and Improved Coordination."

11. Ibid.

12. Ibid.

13. NAIC, "Insurance Department Resources Report," 2005, published in 2007.

14. Andrew Tobias, *The Invisible Bankers: Everything the Insurance Industry Never Wanted You To Know* (New York: Linden Press/Simon & Schuster, 1982).

15. NAIC, "Insurance Department Resources Report," 2005, published in 2007.

16. Ibid.

17. Pennsylvania Insurance Department Press Release, Harrisburg, Pennsylvania, June 23, 1999, quoting Pennsylvania Insurance Commissioner Diane Koken.

18. On March 3, 2000, I interviewed the head of the Consumer Services Bureau of the Pennsylvania Insurance Department and received the responses presented here.

19. Interview with the head of the Consumer Services Bureau of the Pennsylvania Insurance Department, March 3, 2000.

20. According to the NAIC, most states do not make public how many consumers actually benefit monetarily from the insurance department's direct intervention, the amount of the benefit, or what type of claim was pursued. The most information the states do provide is the total amount collected on behalf of consumers.

HEALTHCARECORP

"Putting the 'x' in R"

NOTICE OF CLAIM DENIAL

Dear Insured:

We **regretfully must deny** your claim for medical attention on _____7/29/07_____ because you had one or more of the following **pre-existing conditions:**

☑ You were poor
☑ You were sick

We cheerfully look forward to serving you again at Healthcarecorp, where "The Patients Come First."

Sincerely,

Bea N. Counter

Asst. Claims Reviewer/Profit Maximizer

www.venturacountystar.com/greenberg   steve@greenberg-art.com   VENTURA COUNTY STAR '07 GREENBERG

Healthcare claim denied.
Cartoon by Steve Greenberg, *Ventura County Star*. Reprinted by permission of the artist.

CHAPTER 6

Trends
The Next Decade

"Parts of this industry are literally global, and in a global environment, the current state-based system is just untenable."

— Brian Atchinson, executive director, Insurance Marketplace Standards Association, July 8, 2003

Looking toward the next decade, new problems—national and international trends—are poised to batter the insurance industry, which without any uniform regulatory direction or solution may not be able to contain or guide events.

Brian Atchinson is the former president of the National Association of Insurance Commissioners and a former Maine insurance commissioner. He is now the executive director of the Insurance Marketplace Standards Association (IMSA), an independent, non-profit organization whose mission is to strengthen trust and confidence in the life insurance industry (which includes long-term care and annuity products) by encouraging its member companies to demonstrate commitment to high, ethical standards. Atchinson, an innovative, independent thinker with a good sense of the state of the insurance industry, told me that "There are so many things about state insurance regulation that seem outdated and no longer consistent with where the market has gone. . . . Parts of this industry are literally global, and in a global environment, the current state-based system is just untenable. . . ."

HMOs and Managed Care
Continued Growth and a Continued Stranglehold

The last twenty-five years have seen the delivery of healthcare in the United States turned on its head. As health maintenance organizations (HMOs)—a type of managed care—proliferate, we are seeing the phenomenon of the insurance industry dictating care to the medical profession, instead of the medical profession imposing its needs on the insurance industry. There is no sign that HMOs will disappear in the next ten years, so they need to be controlled.

Doctors have trouble getting paid fully and on time when submitting bills through the HMO. Patients have trouble getting authorization for new procedures, and benefits are dwindling. Insurance bureaucrats are making critical medical decisions. Often, HMO care decisions are based on cost-cutting incentives, not sound medical principles.[1] Looking forward, analysts are predicting that in 2008, we will see the highest health insurance premium rate increases in four years—14.1 percent, up from an 11.7 percent increase in 2007 and a 12.4 percent increase in 2006.[2] On the regulatory side, states seem powerless to control the growth of HMOs or to impose sufficient rules to protect the doctors and the patients.

Numerous stories have surfaced in the media about HMOs denying treatment. For example, an HMO may fail to approve a bone marrow transplant as a treatment for cancer, claiming it is too experimental, although most medical authorities do not consider it to be. Anticipating that an HMO may unilaterally consider bone marrow transplants "experimental," some states such as Florida adopted statutes specifically prohibiting HMOs from excluding coverage for bone marrow transplants recommended by the referring physician and the treating physician, even if there is a policy exclusion for "experimental" procedures.

In December 2007, a California family accused Philadelphia-based HMO insurer CIGNA Corp., of contributing to the death of Nataline Sarkisyan, their 17-year-old leukemia-stricken daughter. She had received a bone marrow transplant from her brother the day before Thanksgiving, but developed a complication, and her liver failed. CIGNA initially denied a liver transplant request, saying it was experimental. After four doctors sent a letter appealing the decision to the insurer, and a large crowd of nurses and community members rallied outside the CIGNA offices in suburban Los Angeles,

CIGNA reversed itself, and agreed to pay for the procedure. However, the young patient died one hour after CIGNA agreed to the procedure. Family attorney Mark Geragos claimed that the insurer "maliciously killed" the teenager, because they did not want to bear the expense of her transplant and aftercare. Geragos said that he intended to ask the Los Angeles district attorney to press murder or manslaughter charges against CIGNA.[3] While many in the legal community did not believe that any criminal charges would be brought, nevertheless the facts received national television attention.

The appeal process for a denied HMO claim can be cumbersome and heavily weighted against the claimant. In some states, such as Pennsylvania, if a claimant whose coverage is denied or terminated wants to appeal, the law allows the claimant's first appeal to be heard by a panel selected by the HMO. A second appeal is allowed, but the panel is again selected by the HMO, although the law allows more specialists to serve on the panel. There is no provision in the law requiring panel members to be independent, and there is no provision allowing claimants to pick an expert to represent them on the panel. Most important, days and months can go by before an HMO claimant can get a decision on whether he or she can have the necessary medical care. While many states are trying to change this stacked-deck approach, it is not a uniform policy shift among all the states.

Polls show that most U.S. citizens do not feel they are getting proper medical attention through HMOs. In a 2007 poll, the public's confidence in HMOs was at only 15 percent.[4]

Healthcare recipients complain that HMOs get away with bad decisions because HMOs and their employer-sponsors are not accountable for the mistakes they make. Many observers believe that the lack of HMO accountability and the anger at the HMO system stems from the Employee Retirement Security Act of 1974 (ERISA). This law prohibits claimants covered under an employer-sponsored healthcare plan from suing the HMO or the employer-sponsor for negligent decision making or negligent care. In addition, under ERISA, the claimant cannot sue for pain and suffering but only for damages equal to the price of the treatment denied.[5] (While ERISA prohibits many people from suing their HMOs and medical directors, not all are shut out by ERISA. Those persons who have individual or non-employer–related insurance programs do not have the ERISA preemption problem, and thus they can sue their HMOs and medical directors.)

According to a 2001 study released by the Kaiser Family Foundation, the biggest impediment to meaningful managed care reform was the impact of the ERISA preemption of suits involving employer-provided healthcare insurance. If this portion of ERISA were repealed and the right to sue an HMO allowed, a major part of the problem would be eliminated. As of the beginning of 2008, the ERISA preemption had not been repealed.

The Kaiser study also noted that the creation of independent review organizations to examine coverage denials implemented by some states as part of the appeal process has gone a long way to eliminate the need for a patient to sue an HMO or other managed care organization.

Suing HMOs and HMO Doctors

A growing number of states, frustrated with ERISA's prohibition of lawsuits against HMOs, circumvented ERISA and passed their own laws allowing suits against the HMOs and employers. This worked well and did not overload the judicial system, as some had feared. The 2001 Kaiser study reported that at the time of the study, in Texas (the first state to allow suits against an HMO) fewer than twenty-five cases had been filed since the state's managed care liability law was passed in September 1997. In Oklahoma, only three suits had been filed; there was one suit in Maine, and none in Arizona, California, Georgia, New Jersey, Washington, and West Virginia.

Unanimous decisions in two companion cases by the U.S. Supreme Court in June 2004 abruptly ended these state laws. The Court ruled that the ERISA preemption, as federal law, was binding on every state, and the Court overturned the Texas law that allowed such suits.[6] Observers point out that by overturning the Texas law, the Supreme Court was really throwing the ball back to Congress to amend or repeal the relevant portion of ERISA.

It is important to note that a person can still sue his/her HMO doctors for malpractice, but not the HMO or the doctors making coverage decisions to withhold treatment. ERISA prevents litigation against doctors making coverage decisions in the administration of a plan, but it does not insulate physicians from accountability to their state licensing agency or association charged to enforce professional standards regarding medical decisions.

Before the 2004 Supreme Court decision, cases attempting to hold HMOs liable for practicing medicine were heard in Texas, Illinois, and other states.[7] In one case, an HMO, United Healthcare, sued the Texas State Board of Medical Examiners in an attempt to overturn the board's strong disciplinary action against the insurer's medical director for refusal to treat a young child. The disciplinary action involved a $5,000 fine, a public reprimand, and a two-year "probated suspension" of the director's medical license. The director could continue to practice but would be required to complete twelve hours of training in the area in which he had denied treatment (an area in which he had no previous experience).

A number of states considered revisions to their codes requiring that doctors working for insurance companies in any capacity (e.g., an in-house medical staff doctor or an outside doctor conducting independent medical exams) be considered to be practicing medicine on that patient, and therefore responsible for their decisions or opinions and subject to the jurisdiction and discipline of the state medical board.

Other cases allowed malpractice claims against an HMO itself, based on a new legal theory of institutional negligence. In one case, an overwhelmed doctor, who was assigned 4,500 patients, had no time to see a baby who subsequently died of bacterial meningitis.[8] The child's condition was diagnosed in the emergency room of the hospital, but although the child's mother thought the condition was serious and attempted to speak with or bring the child in to see his primary care doctor, she was unable to do so. The Illinois Supreme Court decided that the HMO could be held responsible for this tragedy because, according to the court, the HMO assigned the doctor 4,500 patients, a number he couldn't possibly handle.

In addition, HMO insurance executives began to see themselves held administratively accountable if they were found to have handled a claim file directly or even indirectly, intentionally, or with gross recklessness. This means that they could be held responsible for civil (and perhaps even criminal) penalties. The concept of civil and/or criminal penalties applied to corporate executives in certain types of industries is not new; however, it is rarely enforced.

With the U.S. Supreme Court decision of 2004, all this ended. No cases have made inroads beyond that which was in place in 2004. Since 2004, there has been no legislative-based reform of the HMO system, which needs to be reviewed and revised.

For years, there has been a movement in Congress to create a Patients' Bill of Rights, which, among other things, would allow lawsuits for negligence against HMOs, their medical directors, and the employers controlling the plans. While everyone in Congress seems to agree with the other non-controversial rights of patients, the big issue—the right to sue the HMO, the medical directors, and the employers—has consistently run into opposition. As a result, there has been no Patients' Bill of Rights. It is essential that Congress expeditiously address the HMO accountability problem as well as the issue of fair distribution of healthcare.

Insurance Policy "Gotcha"
Insurers' Use of "Independent" Experts

The unregulated use of experts is another ominous trend. Here, a presumably but not actually independent specialist or independent medical expert is selected and paid by the insurer, which then uses the expert's findings to determine the worthiness of the claim. Such experts are used in all parts of the insurance industry—auto, home-owners, and, of course, healthcare.

The insurance policy generally allows the insurance company to require the claimant to be the subject of an independent medical examination (IME) or other independent expert evaluation. It allows the company unilaterally to select an independent medical expert or other expert, and usually does not permit the joint selection of the doctor or other expert by the claimant and insurer. The result is often a biased report in favor of the insurer, which "papers the file" and gives the insurer an excuse to limit, deny, or terminate the claim. While some reports prepared for some carriers are straightforward and accurate, many others are significantly biased.

An exposé in 1998 about claims related to the January 17, 1994, earthquake in Northridge, California, showed that Allstate tried to drastically cut its earthquake claim losses by hiring uncertified engineers who lowballed the estimated costs of repairs. Allstate used these estimates to adopt a take-it-or-leave-it attitude toward the claimants. A story broadcast on ABC-TV's *20/20* focused on two bewildered old women who refused to accept Allstate's settlement offer. Still visible after four years were two-inch-wide cracks running the length of their apartment's floor.[9]

Allstate officials, when confronted with the TV investigation evidence of unlicensed and questionable experts (who used counterfeit engineering stamps affixed to the reports submitted, or otherwise attesting to having a valid license), admitted that their claims handling here was "an unfortunate mistake."[10] Allstate officials never admitted that they knew the experts were unlicensed or that the stamps were counterfeit. While the district attorney promised an investigation, no charges were brought against Allstate, although the "experts" were disciplined.

Story after story has emerged about some insurers' use of biased independent medical examinations and insurer-paid expert reports as justification for denial, termination, or settlement of claims. Witness the thousands of lawsuits, such as those in the late 1990s alleging UnumProvident's denials of disability claims based on the reports of biased doctors. There were also, from 2005 to 2007, thousands of lawsuits regarding Hurricane Katrina, many of which alleged that State Farm used biased engineers in order to deny hurricane claims.

The need is apparent to implement regulations requiring the uniform licensing and periodic recertification of experts and healthcare professionals performing IMEs. This can be done by peer review of their reports, complaints against them, and other reasonable evaluation methods. In addition, doctors acting as independent medical experts must be scrutinized by state medical licensing boards and punished if they are practicing medicine below that state's standard. Further, selecting and paying independent medical experts, professionals, and other experts should be done through a blind pool, or by agreement of both insurer and claimant, and the expert must certify that he/she is independent with no ties to either side.

Insurance Policy "Gotcha"
Trap Door Clauses

An insurance policy is full of complex and surprising clauses, yet hardly anyone ever reads a policy cover to cover, nor does anyone read the supplemental notices sent by the carrier. (If these things are read, they are so complex that many people do not understand their impact.) This sometimes results in a critical consumer awakening when a claim is filed. Added to this equation is the possibility that the insurer experiences an economic downturn or more frequent and expensive claims, and an unsuspecting or under-informed policyholder might discover that the changed language actually reduces the policy's benefits. This trend will likely continue unless and until policies, supplements, and notices are written in "plain English," the public is educated, and regulators carefully review the importance of some of these hidden problems, disapproving a policy with clearly ambiguous, debatable, or misleading terms.

For example, Allstate offered "extended replacement value coverage" to homeowners in the San Diego, California, area. The term was misleading. In 2003, when a huge wildfire known as the Cedar fire destroyed more than 2,200 middle- and upper-class homes and killed fifteen people, homeowners were shocked to find that "extended replacement value coverage" was actually less coverage than the normal "guaranteed replacement coverage." Guaranteed replacement insurance covers rebuilding your home, no matter what the cost. Extended replacement value insurance, on the other hand, covers up to 100 percent of the value of the home at the time of the purchase of the policy *plus* a certain percentage to cover rebuilding the home in today's market.[11] Average consumers, who might not have read the fine print, could easily believe that when Allstate told them it was changing their policy to give them "extended" coverage at no change in premium cost, it meant more, not less, coverage than they had before. This was not the case, however. To illustrate how important this language switch can be, let's assume it will actually cost $450,000 to rebuild your house using today's prices. Let's also assume that the value of your home in the marketplace was at the time of policy purchase only $250,000. You may be offered the market value of the house plus a percentage to rebuild, which could be substantially less than $450,000, if your policy was switched from guaranteed replacement coverage to extended replacement value coverage.

That's what happened to a number of the homeowners whose homes were destroyed in the Cedar fire. When their homes were destroyed, the carrier offered much less than the homeowners needed to rebuild and thought their insurance covered. Once the homeowners started to litigate against the insurer, the homeowners realized that they were up against an army of lawyers, that it would take forever to settle the cases, and that the cases would be subject to appeal, so they caved in and settled for less than half of what they thought they were insured for. Their homes were gone, and their money was gone—and no one was there to protect them.[12]

Next, there are insurance companies that offer a "flexible, adjustable" universal life insurance policy. This appears attractive because it allows the premiums to be flexible, that is, they can be paid to the carrier sporadically (as long as a minimal required amount is paid). The face amount of the insurance can also be adjustable—up or down—so that if, for example, an insured did not need the higher amount of insurance and wanted to reduce his or her premium, the face amount could be adjusted to accommodate the customer's changing estate planning and family budget needs.

The big sleeper in the flexible, adjustable concept—overlooked by the customer and not made clear by the insurer—is that if the policyholder made these changes, there is, in some policies, an expensive "surrender charge" to effectuate the transaction. Surrender charges are intended to deter a customer from cashing in a policy in the early years, while the commission is still being paid to the person who sold the policy. While the flexible, adjustable terms may appear on the front page of the policy, the wording about the surrender charge may not appear until further back in the policy. Once the policyholder recognizes the impact of the surrender charge, he or she can readily grasp the chilling effect it can have on the entire flexibility and adjustability of the policy. The once attractive, flexible, adjustable portion of the policy can be implemented by the customer only at a serious cost, and the customer realizes too late that it is just another sales gimmick.

Then there is the wording used in the State Farm policy and with other insurers that affected so many Katrina claims—the "anti-concurrent causation clause" where wind damage is covered, but not in combination with flood damage. Most policyholders buying protection against hurricane damage never notice this clause.

There are also litigious clauses, such as appeared in some of UnumProvident's disability policies requiring that the claimant receive "appropriate" medical care. After the claimant was treated for a long time, the company could decide unilaterally that the medical care was "inappropriate" and terminate the claim. At that point, if litigation follows, the insurance carrier plays a waiting game knowing that many claimants, thinking about the long road of litigation, choose to settle in frustration, and the insurance company pays out much less on the policy than it might otherwise have.

Unless the regulators insist on more transparency in the wording of policies, the trend toward more and more "gotcha" language will continue.

Demutualization
Shareholders Over Claimants?

It was predicted in 2000 that most mutual life insurers (where the policyholders are the owners of the company, having "mutual" interest) would convert to some form of public ownership, and that demutualization (conversion to a public corporation with outside investors) was going to be one of the leading valuation drivers behind the U.S. life insurance industry. Demutualization is usually done to make access to capital easier, and it is a trend in the insurance industry.[13] It may represent the biggest recorded financial windfall in history.[14] In 2007, the trend toward demutualization continued.

Since 1930, more than 200 mutual life insurance companies have demutualized and distributed more than $100 billion to policy owners. Recent demutualized life insurers include John Hancock, Manufacturers Life, MetLife, Mutual of New York, Phoenix Mutual, Principal, Prudential, and Sun Life. At the end of 2005, there were fewer than eighty mutual life insurers in the United States.[15]

Demutualization works this way: the shareholders of the old mutual insurance company (which was owned by its policyholders, who therefore had a mutual interest in seeing the company fairly operated) are given stock in a new public company that will have outside shareholders. Companies that have gone from straight mutual insurers to straight stock conversions (full demutualization) give the policyholders a fair shake because they give the policyholders a cash stake in the newly converted company. It is the hybrid, known as a mutual holding company (MHC), that appears to be giving policyholders, lawmakers, and the courts the most trouble. A mutual holding company usually has the ability to issue new stock, but it can effectively avoid giving the old policyholders anything except a noncash stake in the company (the right to receive dividends) that can become valuable only if the company later creates a full demutualization.

In an MHC, the old mutual policyholders are pushed aside and are generally powerless, without legal action, to stop the demutualization. The executives are the biggest beneficiaries; the policyholders are the smallest beneficiaries. With the issuance of new ownership interests to outsiders, the old policyholders' power to control the company is greatly diminished, the emphasis on bottom-line profits may negatively affect the company's decisions on paying legitimate claims, and old policyholders do not realize the cash windfall of a full demutualization—the worst of all worlds. As of September 2005, MHCs were permitted in only thirty states and the District of Columbia, and full demutualization was allowed in forty-four states, the District of Columbia, and Puerto Rico.[16]

While demutualization need not be bad, it could become a problem if the current respective regulatory schemes (federal law for banks, federal law for securities, state laws for insurance companies) collide and consumers are caught in the middle without the protection and oversight they need. The demutualization system needs to be uniform, not presided over by forty-four states with different laws and six states without any laws on the subject.

In creating a stock-based company and eliminating mutual ownership, the temptation is always there to create a strong income stream, resulting in increased stock price for the outside investor shareholders, which may come at the expense of the insurance policyholder. The demutualized insurance company must keep in mind the time-honored insurance industry goal of a fair determination of claims. If the newly reconstituted insurance company moves its focus to mainly bottom-line monetary issues, and away from paying legitimate claims, it will significantly erode the cornerstone of insurance: trust.

States have not been able to come up with a uniform plan that will protect the mutual policyholder in every state. Nor have the states been able to instill proper and uniform rules on the newly demutualized company so that the old policyholder isn't hurt.

Medical Malpractice Insurance
A Continuing Crisis

In late 2002 and early 2003, the states of Florida, New Jersey, Nevada, Pennsylvania, West Virginia, and several others were threatened with a physician walkout, motivated by significantly increased malpractice insurance premiums.[17] In February 2006, the American Medical Association (AMA) declared twenty-one states in crisis, alarmed by dramatically increased medical malpractice premiums, veteran doctors closing practices, new doctors refusing to practice in high-premium cities, and doctor boycotts. The number was reduced to seventeen states in 2007.[18] As of 2007, despite reforms aimed at curbing malpractice, the medical malpractice insurance premium crisis had not been resolved, and the trend toward higher premiums continued. Whether people are more litigious, medical providers are deviating more from accepted standards of their specialty, or both, malpractice suits have continued to increase, and premiums continue to go up. For example, a recent survey found that New York hospitals have had their medical malpractice premiums skyrocket, up 175 percent since 2000. This followed the New York State Insurance Department's approval of a 14 percent raise in medical malpractice insurance rates for doctors, which went into effect on July 1, 2007.[19] Media reports document that doctors have left or have threatened to leave their practice, or cause a work stoppage, to avoid what they believe are excessive malpractice premiums. State governments and the individual insurance departments, which in the past may have taken a laissez-faire attitude to the problem, are now working through the myriad issues and pressures that have created the crisis.

According to numerous media and medical association sources, medical malpractice premiums of $200,000 or more per year are being charged to medical specialists, such as obstetrician-gynecologists. The media and the medical associations confirm the dramatic increases in medical malpractice insurance. The premiums have caused sticker shock for even the most casual of observers.

The medical malpractice insurance problem has no easy solution. For every well-documented argument identifying the cause or offering an answer to the dilemma, there is another well-documented position paper stating just the opposite. The insurers blame high jury awards in medical malpractice cases and urge monetary caps on all noneconomic damages (for pain and suffering) in malpractice awards. Firing back are the trial lawyers and consumers, who blame the insurance companies for seizing on a "manufactured" crisis in jury awards to cover up the real problems. The insurers' crisis, they say, is actually a direct result of the insurers' poor investment decisions coupled with shareholder pressure for profits. The attempt to recoup from those poor investments and the pressure for profits were still present in 2007.

According to some observers, one of the most effective ways to control the malpractice insurance crisis is the implementation of "caps" on courtroom awards of noneconomic damages (pain and suffering). California cites its MICRA law (the Medical Injury Compensation Reform Act of 1975), which limits damages for medical malpractice with the use of caps to $250,000 for noneconomic damages (pain and suffering), as being effective. The MICRA law also abrogates the Collateral Source Rule (the rule that prohibits the defense from telling the jury that the plaintiff has recovered or could recover damages from someone else (e.g., an insurer or family member). In addition, MICRA sets a limit on contingent fee payments to lawyers, and allows installment payments (which stop if the plaintiff dies) instead of a lump sum.

On the surface, a cap approach may appear to be a solution. President George W. Bush has expressed the opinion many times that caps on malpractice awards will reduce the number of malpractice lawsuits and the cost of malpractice insurance premiums.

However, on deeper analysis, there are other societal, economic, and legal issues involved with the imposition of caps. Many consumer and legal groups (including major bar associations) say that caps will have a chilling effect on cases requiring proper compensation for devastating, life-altering malpractice injuries (such as when the wrong leg is amputated or breast cancer is misdiagnosed, resulting in an unnecessary double mastectomy). They point out that those who would be hurt the most by caps are infants, the elderly, and the unemployed or underemployed and their families, because our tort litigation system is geared to economic loss (i.e., payment based on work compensation and occupation at the time of the claim projected into the future). They contend that in our current system, noneconomic pain and suffering damages are the great equalizers for those who have no economic damage from the malpractice, but suffer greatly.

Some states that have caps have reported that their medical malpractice premiums have nevertheless gone up significantly. For example, West Virginia has a cap of $1 million for noneconomic damages, yet it is one of the states faced with a physician walkout crisis as a result of increased premiums. In addition, when California imposed its $250,000 cap on noneconomic damages, malpractice insurance premiums at first rose significantly. It took many years before there was any overall reduction in premiums. Other states have reported a similar phenomenon.

The National Conference of State Legislatures, which studied the issue, has stated that while caps may create market stability and predictability of insurer profits, they do not necessarily hold down premiums.[20]

Lawyers usually charge a contingent fee in medical malpractice cases. They get paid only when they win, sometimes after years of time and effort involving research, expenses, legal pleadings, experts, discovery, and, ultimately, trial. Thus—according to conversations I had with several California lawyers—when presented with a significant case that has limited monetary recovery possibilities because of the cap, lawyers are turning away meritorious cases.

Doctors, on the other hand, blame the legal system for allowing overzealous lawyers to besmirch their reputations, and they accuse lawyers of overreaching. According to the AMA, if it were not for the huge jury verdicts and large out-of-court settlements against doctors, the current crisis would not exist.

Studies show that million-dollar "runaway" court verdicts are relatively rare. Other studies reveal that medical malpractice awards are actually a very small part of the overall amount of money collected in annual premiums by insurers. Still other investigations reveal that the amount of large malpractice verdicts against doctors is actually going down.[21]

Thus, the lawyers claim that insurers' criticism of high jury verdicts is a smokescreen and that the insurers are trying to bail themselves out of bad investment portfolios with higher malpractice premiums. According to trial lawyers, the malpractice crisis is a cyclical problem, and premiums will drop only when the investment market turns around. They point out that in the mid-1980s, the same thing happened: Insurers raised malpractice insurance premiums because of a bad investment market, and rates later came down when the investment market stabilized.[22] Insurers strongly disagree. They say that they have not invested in anything speculative, have sufficient money to pay claims, and act with an evenhanded approach to claims handling and shareholder profits. Whether one believes the lawyers or the insurers, the fact is that the stock market has gone up steadily, and medical malpractice insurance rates are still going up.

One highly publicized study by the Institute of Medicine (part of the National Academy of Sciences) in 1999 claimed that there were more than 98,000 deaths each year due to hospital error. A 2004 study of 37 million patient records in the United States doubled that figure to an average of 195,000 potentially preventable in-hospital deaths resulting from medical errors in each of the years 2000–2002.[23] The watchdog group Public Citizen noted that only 5.4 percent of doctors are responsible for 56.2 percent of medical malpractice payments, and more than 80 percent of doctors in the United States have never had a claim settled against them.[24,25] If that is the case, informed consumers wonder why the states, through their medical review boards, and the doctors themselves, through medical and other associations, have taken few or no steps to weed out the apparently small group of doctors who keep committing malpractice.

Additional studies have shown that the impact of medical malpractice awards on the overall cost of insurance is overblown, and that the amount and severity of malpractice damage awards have declined substantially between 1990 and 2005. A Harvard study in 2006 indicated that the cost of malpractice lawsuits—including legal fees, insurance costs, and payouts—comes to less than one-half of 1 percent of healthcare spending.[26]

In the middle of this mess is the average citizen who needs to understand that bad results do not necessarily mean malpractice, and that filing a malpractice lawsuit does not necessarily mean being awarded a large amount of money.

Solutions to the Medical Malpractice Insurance Crisis

As stated above, many solutions have been suggested to cure the medical malpractice insurance crisis. Some have to do with an internal reorganization of the thinking and administration in medical and hospital practices. For example, in the book *Internal Bleeding: The Truth Behind America's Terrifying Epidemic of Medical Mistakes,*[27] the authors—both medical doctors—stated that in addition to the legal problems in the medical arena, there are other egregious but fixable medical problems that could result in fewer malpractice claims. Among the solutions posed are the elimination of sloppy "patient handoffs" (failing to communicate about the patient from doctor to doctor, or from hospital to hospital, and permutations thereof) and "negligent read-backs" (failing to double-check prescriptions or dosages, or failing to check medical charts to make certain the correct patient is being treated).[27]

Other suggestions relate to regulatory reforms. As a close observer of the industry for many years, I offer the following summary of ideas (my own and those of others) for solving the medical malpractice crisis, some of which have already been implemented through state insurance regulations:

- Easier regulatory approval process for qualified insurers

- Closer review and audit of insurers

- Stricter medical peer review

- Creation of statewide malpractice insurance case adjudication programs

- Stronger consumer advocacy

- "Certificate of merit" (doctor affidavit filed in court saying malpractice was committed) and venue requirements (no forum shopping to file lawsuit in the best verdict counties)

- Stronger penalties for frivolous lawsuits

- Creation of "Certified Medical Malpractice" attorneys (passing special exam)

- Caps on annual premium increases

- Insurance premium discounts or other incentives for doctors with no claims or minimum claims

- Freezing of premiums for a limited time

- Obtaining insurer commitment to stay in the state (tax incentives, other programs)

- Implementation of nationwide standards instead of local or community standards for medical care

Other solutions could be implemented, but they may be less likely to solve the problem. These include:

- Implementation of a voluntary "no fault" medical malpractice system

- Adding another state-funded "layer" of standby insurance

It is clear that the solution to the medical malpractice crisis lies with government and its regulation, and nowhere else. While many other groups can assist, a nongovernmental organization cannot itself solve the problem. The government must take the lead. The state governments, through their insurance departments, need to tighten their scrutiny of all sides of the medical malpractice arena and create a win-win situation for insurers, doctors, claimants, lawyers, the court system, and the public alike.

Each governor and state legislature, with the input of each state insurance commissioner and insurance department experts (including a consumer advocate), need to come together to address the issue with all of the parties and reach a democratic, truly representative consensus. The governors and their insurance departments, or the state legislatures, as well intentioned as they might be, could conceivably come up with fifty different solutions. However, by the time the medical malpractice matter gets resolved in all fifty states, one by one, it will be too late: Our healthcare system could deteriorate and patients needing immediate medical care could be turned away.

Terrorism and Natural Disasters
Government Backstops?

The terrorist attacks on September 11, 2001, on the World Trade Center and the Pentagon, as well as the downing of the plane in western Pennsylvania, had reverberations in the insurance industry that changed the insurance landscape, probably forever. Terrorism insurance loss estimates for the 9/11 attacks were in the area of $93 billion.[28] Facing huge claims, insurers announced that in the future, they would refuse to insure open-ended risks without federal help.

After 9/11, insurers balked at the cost of terrorism coverage for tall buildings or other potential targets. Insurers told Congress that the U.S. government needed to make a long-term commitment to terrorism coverage. They claimed that the uncertainty over insurance coverage for terrorism causes massive cascading problems, not only for the insurers, who are reluctant to insure against this almost unquantifiable risk, but also for the reinsurers onto whom the risk is shifted. The insurers also said that financial institutions would insist more than ever that all risks for which they lend money are insured against terrorism attacks.

Terrorism also presents a big problem to consumers and businesses. A borrower—whether it is an individual, a business, a real estate entity, or some other—that fails to have adequate insurance (including terrorism insurance) may find itself in default on loan covenants, may cause the loan to be called for immediate repayment, and might even find itself in financial jeopardy.

In late 2001 and 2002, the reaction of the insurance industry was swift. Several large property and casualty insurers, including AIG and Chubb, testified before Congress and presented something like an ultimatum to the U.S. government: Either take a major layer of our insurance risk in the form of a federally guaranteed insurance program, or we will not continue to write terrorism coverage.

When hearings were held in late 2001 by the House Committee on Financial Services, Representative Richard H. Baker (R, Louisiana)—the chair of the Subcommittee on Capital Markets, Insurance, and Government Sponsored Enterprises—and other lawmakers asked the insurers why the federal government should take a layer of the risk when the federal government has no audit, oversight, or regulatory power over the insurance industry under current law.[29] Several representatives were opposed to the federal government taking this level of risk and were "extremely reluctant to accept any plan that puts the taxpayer on the hook for insurable losses [particularly] when there is no federal office that exercises any real jurisdiction over solvency and business practices of the industry."[30] The same question was raised in the Senate.[31]

In November 2002, President Bush signed the Terrorism Risk Insurance Act of 2002 (TRIA) into law. The act failed to address the significant question of federal oversight of the insurance industry. TRIA created two layers of insurance. Insurers would take the risk from the first dollar up to $12 billion. Over that, the federal government would cover the risk up to $100 billion. After $100 billion, the insurers pick up the rest. The legislation also required that all commercial insurers offer terrorism coverage. TRIA was limited to a three-year period, until the end of 2005. (TRIA took no position on the McCarran-Ferguson Act.)

As of early 2003, most businesses were not buying the terrorism insurance because it was either too expensive or they did not see themselves as potential targets. In 2004, several groups were urging continuation of TRIA, while others opposed to the law believed it was an unnecessary bailout. A Consumer Federation of America study in November 2002 indicated that the insurers could withstand a major terrorism claim well above the levels at which the government (taxpayer) level would attach. The CFA further noted that the insurers intended to use this "subsidy" for their own benefit and that they would not return any of the government money to policyholders or taxpayers. TRIA renewal was endorsed by then Federal Reserve Board Chair Alan Greenspan; it was opposed by then Secretary of the Treasury John Snow.

After much debate, Congress extended TRIA to December 2007. (In late 2007, the House passed a bill extending the law for another fifteen years; the Senate passed a different version, and as of this writing, a compromise bill had not been voted upon.) Even as an extension was being discussed, however, many in Congress were asking the same question: Shouldn't the federal government have oversight of how the insurers administer this program? At present, the federal government has no such ability to audit the insurers to verify whether such funds would be used properly. Will Congress walk a wide berth around the McCarran-Ferguson Act again?

Natural Disaster Insurance: A Government Layer?

In April and June 2007, Congress held hearings on a new issue: whether the federal government should create a fund to assist and incentivize private enterprise insurers, to cover homeowners and businesses for catastrophic natural disasters (floods, hurricanes, wildfires, mudslides, earthquakes, and drought) that could occur in any part of the country. This concept arose out of the massive denials of Hurricane Katrina homeowners and business claims, and the reluctance of insurers to continue to insure in catastrophe-prone areas. The concept was essentially the same as the Terrorism Risk

Insurance Act: The federal government would take a layer of catastrophe insurance above the private insurers' layer. The issue of federal backstopping of private enterprise insurers without the ability to oversee the use of the funds was raised in testimony submitted before Senate and House committees. The issue of federal oversight is being considered and will no doubt be raised again.

The Sale of Insurance on the Internet
Financial Modernization vs. the Wild West

The specter of insurance being sold on the Internet without uniform federal regulation has the potential to become a big problem—the equivalent of going into uncharted territory with no controls.

Companies regularly pop up on the Internet offering a smorgasbord of insurance products: auto, homeowners, term life, individual health, disability income, renters, long-term care, small business, annuities, motorcycle, whole life, medical, dental, workers compensation, boat, and so forth. Insurers selling on the Internet once conjured up thoughts of fly-by-night companies and generated hearty suspicion. However, it is clear now that very big companies are involved in Internet insurance sales, so an air of credibility and confidentiality has been established. The entries into the market include some major names in the insurance world. Personal automobile insurance is being sold on the Internet by sellers like State Farm, Allstate, Progressive, GEICO, and Nationwide. Life insurance sellers include AIG, MetLife, Northwestern Mutual, Prudential, and New York Life. Individual health insurance sellers include UnitedHealth, WellPoint, Kaiser Permanente, and Aetna.[32]

Studies indicate that the Web has become an increasingly important communications channel between sellers and buyers of personal insurance and that most consumers' purchasing process is Webinfluenced. Pure online sales are growing. While in 2007, Internet insurance sales accounted for less than 15 percent of sales (even of personal auto insurance), predictions are that online insurance sales will double by 2011 to about 30 percent. It is also predicted that the Web will play a major role in most personal insurance purchases across auto, life, and health insurance.[33] Billions of dollars will be transacted in cyberspace, whether it is for advertising, promotion, information, administration, or sales.

Compounding the problem is the Gramm-Leach-Bliley Act of 1999 (GLB), which repealed the Prohibition-era Glass-Steagall Act, which prohibited banks, insurance companies, and stock brokerage companies from going outside their specific area of business. Now, all three may cross over into the others' territories and participate in, merge with, and acquire the others' business.

As a result, among other things, insurance companies and brokerage firms are now creating banks and lending money, and banks are now advertising on the Internet to sell insurance. Since the GLB requires banks and brokerage companies to remain under federal law, and insurance to remain under state law, the question arises as to which law applies if a bank runs into trouble while selling insurance on the Internet—federal or state.

Under Section 304 of the GLB, in case of a regulatory conflict between state (insurance) and federal (banking, securities) jurisdictions, regulators can seek expedited judicial review by the U.S. Court of Appeals for the jurisdiction in which the state is located, or in the U.S. Court of Appeals for the District of Columbia. The act says the court must look at the state and federal regulatory conflicts "without unequal deference"; it is unclear what that means. Further, the act preserves the Federal Reserve Board's central role as the umbrella regulator of all companies that own banks. Unless the GLB is amended, the courts will have to sort it out.[34]

The best advice is *caveat emptor*: Let the buyer beware. Even with some of the larger companies striving for privacy and confidentiality, buying insurance on the Internet could subject the unwary customer to fraudulent schemes: imposter websites (websites that look like the real site but take the private information and use it illegally, without the knowledge of the applicant), sale of worthless insurance (e.g., a fictitious company offering a small business health insurance plan or workers compensation coverage at a low rate), or sale of policies unlicensed in the customer's state.

The sale of insurance on the Internet is therefore another trend requiring federal, not state, oversight. Currently, purchase of insurance is available without respect to which state has jurisdiction or which state governs the offering, sale, or taxation of the insurance. Whether premium tax revenue is being collected, and by whom, is another question to be resolved.

Since the Internet has no geographic boundary, no one state has jurisdiction. Therefore, if there is a claim problem, the consumer may have only minimal redress. The rapid growth of computer technology has transformed the world into one global economy in which U.S. and alien insurers compete. If the insurer is from another country, the consumer may have even less protection. No cases have arisen yet, but once they arrive, courts and legislators will realize the enormous problems the Internet presents. At present, the states cannot even begin to deal with the Internet. The federal government is just now starting to wrestle with the global legal impact of the Internet. If properly controlled, the Internet may indeed be a benefit for insurance consumers. If it is uncontrolled, the Internet may pose serious problems.

Long-Term Care
A Problem Looming on the Horizon

People are living longer. Our population is aging, and many people are living late into their eighties and nineties. In fact, some life insurance customers are asking brokers or agents for a premium quote and an illustration through 110 years old. In 2007, the average life expectancy for an American baby born in 2004 was 77.9 years,[35] and most likely the average life expectancy will be going higher.

Estimates reveal that two of every five Americans over the age of sixty-five will spend time in a nursing home. The newest insurance product to arrive on the scene, therefore, is private long-term care insurance. Long-term care insurance pays for the cost of daily care for persons with long-term illness or disability. Different plans offer flexible options, including home healthcare, alternate care facilities (such as assisted living facilities), nursing home care, and adult day care. While estimates are that only 5 percent of those over sixty-five currently have private long-term care insurance, it has been reported that more than 100 insurance companies are now offering such policies.

Senior citizens with all their vulnerabilities are fertile territory for abuse. Possible insurance abuse in this area needs to be carefully and uniformly watched since the elderly are least likely, financially and emotionally, to be able to prosecute a contested claim and litigate against a large carrier. Nor are seniors likely to be able to safeguard their rights. A fee-only insurance adviser in Michigan has stated that "Long-term care is the big hustle in the insurance industry."[36]

Senior citizens holding these long-term care policies could easily become victims of the vulture culture and be forced to litigate in order to receive insurance payments. If so, there may be additional complications. Often in a long-term care scenario, the victim's health continues to deteriorate to the point where the person might be physically incapable of assisting his or her attorney in fighting the insurance companies.

Consider the case of Mary Rose Derks of Conrad, Montana. Derks, a widow, was highlighted in a *New York Times* article in March 2007 that exposed the problems with long-term care insurance.[37] The article excoriated Conseco, a long-term care insurance carrier, for turning down a claim from Derks. Every month since she had reached the age of sixty-five in 1990, she had pulled together $100 for a long-term care insurance policy that would pay for a place in an assisted living home when she needed it.

In 2002, after serious bouts with hypertension and diabetes and many hospitalizations, she checked into a state-licensed nursing home near her daughter's home. Conseco turned down her claim, first saying that she waited too long to file the claim. Then, the carrier said the facility was not approved, despite its state license. Finally, the company argued that Derks was not sufficiently ill, despite her early-stage dementia and the three dozen pills she took each day. According to the article, Derks, now 81, has yet to receive a penny from Conseco. Each time she sent in more information to the carrier, she received the same response: claim denied.

Conseco responded to media inquiries by stating that it "is committed to the highest standards for ethics, fairness and accountability, and strives to pay all claims in accordance with the policy contracts." The *New York Times* indicated that it had reviewed more than 400 of the thousands of grievances and lawsuits filed in recent years, against carriers selling long-term care insurance, which showed elderly policyholders confronting unnecessary delays and overwhelming bureaucracies. The article stated that in California alone, one in every four long-term care claims was denied by the carriers in 2005.

The entire area of long-term care insurance needs to be carefully and uniformly regulated. Yet these insurers are regulated in the same patchwork manner as other areas of insurance, that is, by the fifty nonuniform states. In some states, the legislature has adopted the NAIC's model legislation for long-term care insurance.[38] In other states, the model legislation has not been adopted, but some form of regulation exists. In still others, the laws are negligible on this subject. There is no legislated, uniform regulatory set of rules to follow. So the climate is ripe for problems.

Commendably, the NAIC's model legislation for long-term care insurance has made the act of post-claim underwriting illegal. Post-claim underwriting occurs when an insurer has failed to do a satisfactory independent investigation before issuing a policy; when a claim comes in, the insurer revisits the claimant's history in search of negative information in order to avoid payment. Notwithstanding this prohibition, the act of post-claim underwriting is still attempted.

For example, in *Schneider v. Unum*, Unum was sued for refusing to pay a long-term care insurance claim and for engaging in post-claim underwriting. Unum filed a motion to dismiss the case, saying that under ERISA the claimant was precluded from suing. The U.S. District Court refused to dismiss the case against the disability insurer. If the facts were proved, the court said, it could amount to a violation of the state's long-term care insurance law.[39]

Schneider, the claimant, was enrolled for long-term care insurance during an open enrollment period (a limited period of time during which everyone in a group willing to pay the premium is accepted) offered by the carrier for his teachers' union. Schneider twice told the insurer that he had multiple sclerosis. He made full disclosure on his application. He was told verbally and in writing that he had been approved for the long-term care coverage. He received a certificate of long-term care insurance from the carrier. Premiums were fully paid.

Three years later after he enrolled, Schneider's multiple sclerosis rendered him disabled and in need of benefits, yet he was denied long-term care coverage by the carrier. The carrier said that the policy never took effect. In addition, the carrier said that coverage was denied on the basis of looking back in Schneider's application and finding that he was suffering from multiple sclerosis. According to the carrier, multiple sclerosis would make him totally disabled under the carrier's definitions under the policy, and therefore ineligible for long-term care insurance, and/or in violation of one of the policy's exclusions.

The court did rule that the long-term care insurance plan came under ERISA, and therefore certain of the insured's claims (state common law contract claims and consumer protection claims) were preempted. Nevertheless, the court decided that the state's insurance code (including the prohibition against post-claim underwriting) was not preempted by ERISA. Therefore, the claimant's facts, if proved at trial, could amount to post-claim underwriting and the insurer could suffer significant penalties.[40] Therefore, Unum's motion to dismiss the case was denied by the court.

The facts in the Schneider case are important in that they foreshadow major problems in the administration and sale of long-term care insurance: the approval of sales and marketing of the policy, the interpretation of ambiguous language in the policy, the lack of an expeditious process by which the claimant can get his or her benefits if wrongly delayed or denied, and the regulatory oversight and enforcement or lack thereof. The federal court ruling in the Schneider case indicated the concern that the judicial system had regarding the abuses that could occur in the long-term care insurance area. It should be a signal to insurers that this area will be closely watched.

Properly regulated and properly priced, long-term care insurance could be well worth the cost for some consumers. There are many excellent insurers involved in long-term care that are striving to bring a quality long-term care insurance policy to the consumer, at a fair price and reasonable terms. But the key will be how regulators monitor this new area, so that when problems arise (as they are apt to do) we will have a body of fair and uniform laws in place to protect our seniors.

Here is the next logical question: If different states handle re-underwriting and other regulations for health insurance differently, how does this affect the long-term care policyholder who becomes seriously ill and is faced with higher premiums, the denial of claims, and the prospect of costly and extended litigation against the insurer? Protections for long-term care policyholders should not have to depend on the luck of the draw as to whether you live in a pro-consumer state or not. A uniform set of regulations applicable to all states should be created. Right now there is none.

■ ■ ■

The trends and developments in the insurance industry are bigger than one state can handle or change. Reading through these problem areas and trends should lead one to conclude that the fifty states, under current conditions—no matter how well intentioned they may be—simply cannot individually regulate, administer, and oversee the insurance industry in this changing climate.

Notes

1. Numerous articles reviewing the HMO system conclude that HMOs are designed primarily to cut costs. For example, see *Introduction to Sociology/Health and Medicine* (Wikibooks, August 2007), en.wikibooks.org/wiki/Introduction_to_Sociology/Health_and_Medicine.
2. BLR (Business and Legal Reports), "HMOs Propose Higher Rate Increases," www.compensation.BLR.com, July 2, 2007, quoting Hewitt Associates, a consulting firm.
3. See, for example, "Coverage for bone marrow transplant procedures," 2007 Florida statutes, title 37, insurance, chapter 627, section 627.4236; Alicia Chang, AP Science Writer, "Calif. family blames HMO in girl's death," December 21, 2007, http://news.yahoo.com/s/ap/20071222/ap_on_re_us/teen_liver_transplant.
4. "Confidence in Institutions," Gallup poll, June 11–14, 2007.
5. Employee Retirement Income Security Act (ERISA) of 1974, 29 U.S.C. 1002 (1) et sequitur.
6. *Aetna Health, Inc. et al. v. Juan Davila, et al.* and companion case, *CIGNA Healthcare of Texas, Inc. v. Ruby R. Calad, et al.*, both decided June 21, 2004 by a unanimous U.S. Supreme Court.

7. *New York Times*, May 28, 2000.

8. *Jones v. Chicago HMO Ltd. of Illinois* (Illinois Supreme Court No 86830, Agenda 15), decided May 18, 2000.

9. Brian Ross, "Allegations against Allstate after L.A. Quake," *20/20 Wednesday*, ABC-TV, October 14, 1998.

10. Ross, "Allegations Against Allstate."

11. Dana Dratch, "Home Buyers Guide," www.Bankrate.com, March 15, 2004.

12. "Home Insurance 9-1-1," transcript of *NOW*, PBS-TV, August 17, 2007; see also David Dietz and Darrell Preston, "Home Insurers Secret Tactics Cheat Fire Victims, Hike Profits," *Bloomberg Markets Magazine*, August 3, 2007.

13. "Demutualization," *Barron's Financial and Investment Dictionary*.

14. "Life Insurance Demutualization Primer Available," Smithbarneyresearch .com, January 31, 2000.

15. For an update on the reorganization status of Mutual Life Insurance Companies, see www.glenndaily.com/mhctable.htm, July 2007; see also "Demutualization," www.Answers.com, August 2007.

16. "Demutualization," www.insurance–finance.com, September 11, 2005.

17. Among the numerous newspaper accounts, see, for example, Josh Goldstein, "Two Plans to End the Malpractice Crisis," *Philadelphia Inquirer*, February 2, 2003, and Joseph P. Treaster, "Pennsylvania Physicians Won't Walk Off Jobs," *New York Times*, January 1, 2003.

18. In February 2006, the American Medical Association identified twenty-one states in crisis. They were Arkansas, Connecticut, Florida, Georgia, Illinois, Kentucky, Massachusetts, Mississippi, Missouri, Nevada, New Jersey, New York, North Carolina, Ohio, Oregon, Pennsylvania, Rhode Island, Tennessee, Washington, West Virginia, and Wyoming. In March 2007, the AMA removed four states (Arkansas, Georgia, Mississippi, and West Virginia) from the list due to acceptable tort reform. See also, "State of liability," amednews.com, March 5, 2007, accessible at http://www.ama-assn.org/amednews/2007/03/05/ prca0305.htm.

19. Elizabeth Solomon, "Premiums Skyrocket in 'Broken' Malpractice System," *New York Sun*, August 3, 2007, which cited a Greater New York Hospital Association survey.

20. Cheye Calvo (director, State-Federal Relations Committee of the National Conference of State Legislatures), in a speech to the Pennsylvania House Democratic Policy Committee, televised on PCN (Pennsylvania Cable Network), February 28, 2003.

21. *Public Citizen Report on Malpractice Awards*, January 2007.

22. See, for example, testimony of James Mundy, past president of the Pennsylva-

nia Trial Lawyers Association, to the Pennsylvania Senate Banking and Insurance Committee, March 2003.

23. "In-Hospital Deaths From Medical Errors at 195,000 Per Year in USA," *Medical News Today*, August 9, 2004, which cited a 2004 study released by Health-Grades, an independent healthcare quality rating company, and the Institute of Medicine's 1999 report.

24. "Medical Malpractice Briefing Book: Challenging the Misleading Claims of the Doctors' Lobby," *Public Citizen Report*, August 2004.

25. *Public Citizen Report on Malpractice Awards*, January 2007; see also "The Medical Malpractice Myth," *Slate Magazine*, July 11, 2006, quoting Tom Baker, *The Medical Malpractice Myth* (Chicago: University of Chicago, 2005), and a study by the Harvard School of Public Health and Brigham and Women's Hospital, May 10, 2006.

26. A study by the Harvard School of Public Health and Brigham and Women's Hospital, May 10, 2006.

27. Robert M. Wachter and Kaveh G. Shojania, *Internal Bleeding: The Truth Behind America's Terrifying Epidemic of Medical Mistakes* (New York: Rugged Land, 2004).

28. Robert H. Jerry II, "Insurance, Terrorism and 9/11," *Tort Source,* vol. 5., no. 2, Winter 2003. On March 11, 2002, CNBC-TV reported that the industry increased terrorism insurance loss estimates to $52 billion. Add approximately $41 billion in noninsured losses, and the economic losses resulting from 9/11 were predicted to be in the neighborhood of $93 billion.

29. Joseph B. Treaster, "Insurers Ask Help to Survive Future Losses," *New York Times*, September 27, 2001.

30. Treaster, "Insurers Ask Help."

31. Stephen Labaton, "Bush Advisors Press for Help for Insurers—Want U.S. to Pick Up Costs of Future Terror," *New York Times*, October 25, 2001.

32. Celent Report, "Online Insurance Sales and Marketing: What's Happening and What's Next," Boston, Massachusetts, July 17, 2007.

33. Celent Report, "Online Insurance Sales."

34. Financial Services Modernization Act of 1999, 15 U.S.C. § 6801, et seq., November 12, 1999.

35. U.S. Census Bureau and National Center for Health Statistics, 2007.

36. Jonathan Clements, "How Much Insurance Is Needed to Help Cover Long-Term Care?" *Wall Street Journal Online*, January 29, 2002, quoting Peter Katt, a fee-only life insurance advisor based in Michigan.

37. Charles Duhigg, "Aged, Frail and Denied Care by Their Insurers," *New York Times*, March 26, 2007.

38. See National Association of Insurance Commissioners' Model Legislation for Long-Term Care Insurance, as periodically revised; NAIC's Long-Term Care Insurance Model Act 6400.

39. *Schneider v. UNUM Life Insurance Company of America*, 149 F.Supp.2d 169 (No 00-CV-1838, USDC, E.D. Pa 2001). The District Court in the Third Circuit tackled the issue of whether the insurer violated the provision in the Pennsylvania state code, Section 89. 908, prohibiting post-claim underwriting in long-term care insurance. The court refused to grant total summary judgment to UNUM, stating that notwithstanding the ERISA preemption against bringing state claims, the plaintiff, a multiple sclerosis sufferer, could bring his claim to trial on the basis of the state provision prohibiting post-claim underwriting.

40. Chad Terhune, "Health Insurer's Premium Practices Add to Profit Surge, Roil Customers," *Wall Street Journal*, April 9, 2002.

Fighting the Goliath HMOs. HMOs overwhelming the healthcare system—A fair fight?
Cartoon by John Pritchett. Reprinted with permission of the artist.

CHAPTER 7

The Public Uproar and a Crescendo of Distrust

"If they [the insurance company] can treat a senior member of Congress like that, with the level of influence I have, imagine what they can do to the little guy."

> —Representative John Dingell, Jr. (D, Michigan) on being denied a health
> claim, July 26, 2001

"It's despicable not to make good-faith offers to everybody. . . . Money managers [for the insurance companies] have taken over this whole industry. Their eyes are not on people [Hurricane Katrina claimants] who are hurt, but on the bottom line for the next quarter."

> —J. Robert Hunter, Insurance Director, Consumer Federation of America,
> August 17, 2007

Dingell's Healthcare Crusade

In 2000, U.S. Representative John Dingell, Jr. (D, Michigan), at the age of seventy-four, was advised by his aide that insurance authorization for an inpatient procedure the congressman had had done on his broken ankle was denied. Denied! Several irate phone calls later from Dingell's doctor to the managed care plan, the claim was approved.[1] The incident resonated. Dingell's father, John Dingell, Sr., was diagnosed with tuberculosis at the age of twenty, when he was a printer in Dearborn, Michigan. Uninsured, he had been fired from his job, sent to a sanatorium, and left to die. The senior Dingell survived, became active in politics, and was elected to Congress. In 1943, he introduced the first national health insurance law, but it failed to gain enough congressional support to pass. He died in 1955, after serving twenty-three years in office.

John Dingell, Jr. has been concerned for years about every aspect of the insurance industry. The chair of the House Committee on Energy and Commerce, he is considered one of the longest and leading proponents of an increased federal regulatory role over the insurance industry. In 1991, Dingell's congressional committee introduced a study entitled "Failed Promises," which criticized the National Association of Insurance Commissioners (NAIC) and the state insurance regulators, saying the system under which the states are in control of the industry was weak. The study recommended a major federal overhaul of the insurance industry, especially in the area of solvency.

In 1992 and 1993, Dingell introduced legislation, entitled the Federal Insurance Solvency Act, to establish national standards for state insurance departments to enforce. The act failed to be enacted. In 1994, his committee issued "Wishful Thinking," a sequel to "Failed Promises," calling for national solvency standards and federal regulation of foreign reinsurers.

Dingell's observations and predictions have been chillingly accurate. Dingell believes that the way the insurance system is regulated, with fifty state insurance commissioners heading, in effect, fifty fiefdoms, is Byzantine. He is concerned that under the current insurance system, uniformity among the states is the exception, not the rule.[2]

Every year, from the time he took over his father's congressional seat in late 1955, Dingell has introduced a bill to provide national healthcare to the uninsured. In 2007, the congressman again introduced legislation to create a Patients' Bill of Rights that would allow lawsuits against HMOs and would require insurer accountability and other protections for the consumer against improper actions by insurance companies. While these bills have yet to pass, bipartisan support is finally building for Dingell's crusade.

Dingell's concern about the insurance industry is finally being heard. After Hurricane Katrina, the average citizen is becoming much more aware of the impact that insurance has on one's life. The public has put insurance at the top of the national domestic political agenda.

Shout Out for a Patients' Bill of Rights and the Right to Sue an HMO

The domination of the healthcare scene by HMO health insurers, their sometime denial of needed medical attention (for example, on the grounds that a treatment is experimental or facilities are overutilized), and the need to eliminate the ERISA preemption and give consumers the right to sue HMOs and their medical directors has precipitated public demand for a uniform federal Patients' Bill of Rights.[3]

Most states have statutory protections to ensure fair treatment of consumers and patients accessing healthcare insurance. However, millions of Americans do not enjoy the protection of state law because they are enrolled under an employer-sponsored health plan, and those plans are organized under the federal ERISA laws, which are not subject to state-enacted patient and consumer protections. Consequently, those employees have no safeguards to protect them against health plan abuses, and they cannot sue their HMO and its representatives for denial of care or other problems. Consumers are now demanding a Patients' Bill of Rights.

The term "Patients' Bill of Rights" is a generic one, but at its core are certain basic principles, among them:

1. Emergency room access ("prudent layperson test")—person of average knowledge of health and medicine, could reasonably expect the absence of immediate medical attention to the individual to result in serious jeopardy.)
2. Access to out-of-network providers
3. The ability of specialists to be primary care providers
4. Standing referrals to specialists
5. Direct access to obstetricians and gynecologists
6. Continuity of care when a physician leaves the plan
7. Independent external review of complaints
8. Disclosure of treatment options
9. Prohibition of financial incentives to deny care
10. Independent consumer assistance
11. Access to all prescription drugs
12. Access to clinical trials
13. The right to sue for damages

Of the thirteen items, by far the most contentious is the last one, giving the claimant the right to sue an HMO for damages, which would require the repeal of the ERISA preemption. Advocates of a Patients' Bill of Rights, such as the nonprofit, nonpartisan group Families USA, urge the inclusion of all thirteen as part of basic patients' rights legislation.

There is almost 100 percent unanimity about the need for the passage of a federal Patients' Bill of Rights. Yet every bill has stalled in Congress. Both the House and Senate have at different times separately passed similar patient protection bills, but as of late 2007, no such legislation has been enacted into law. In February 2007— shortly before he died—Representative Charlie Norwood (R, Georgia), a champion of the cause to enact a comprehensive Patients' Bill of Rights bill, joined John Dingell in sponsoring H.R. 979, the newest version of the Patients' Bill of Rights. The House had yet to discuss the bill as of late 2007, and the Senate had yet to introduce a corresponding bill. In the past, the reason the bill has failed to pass is that if the right to sue the HMO and the employer-sponsor is accepted, the insurance companies want a cap on the noneconomic (pain and suffering) damages that can be assessed against the insurer or administrators. The issue of the cap might still be an obstacle.

Polls Plus Hard Facts Demonstrate Public Displeasure

For the past ten years, national polling firms and government statistical analysts have documented the rise in insurance costs and the public's adverse reaction to insurance in general and healthcare insurance in particular.

Just the Facts

The cost of family health insurance has skyrocketed 81 percent since 2000. Premiums are rising twice as fast as wages and inflation. The

typical middle-class family health insurance premium is now
$11,480 a year, compared with $6,348 in 2000.[4] Today, persons
under the age of twenty-five spend 2.5 percent of their total annual
expenditures on healthcare, and those sixty-five and older spend five
times that amount—12.8 percent of their total spending. Today, the
average annual expenditure for healthcare is 5.7 percent, plus 11.2
percent for personal insurance and pensions, totaling 16.9 percent
of an average consumer's budget. (The big four expenses are housing, 32.7 percent; transportation, 18 percent; insurance, 16.9 percent; and food, 12.8 percent.)[5] The number of Americans without
health insurance rose to a record high in 2005. The number of uninsured Americans has increased every year since 2000, from 39.8 million that year to 46.6 million in 2005. It now stands at 47 million.[6]

The Polls

Fifty-six percent of Americans believe that fundamental changes are
needed in our healthcare system, and 34 percent believe that we have
to completely rebuild the system.[7] Fifty-five percent believe that the
U.S. healthcare system has major problems, and 16 percent say it's
in a state of crisis.[8] Sixty-four percent believe that the government
should provide a national health insurance program for all Americans, even if it would require higher taxes.[9]

The polls all the way back to 1998 carried the same message. The
pollsters (*Washington Post*/ABC Poll, *Newsweek* Poll, Harris Poll,
CBS News/*New York Times* Poll, Gallup/CNN/*USA Today* Poll)
have consistently shown that a majority of consumers are very critical of the health insurance industry in particular, and the insurance
industry in general, and feel that stronger regulation of the industry
is needed now. The ten-year span of polls shows that the public level
of discontent regarding insurance has not diminished.

In a 1998 *Washington Post* poll, more than 86 percent of those
responding had some form of health insurance (fee for service,
HMO, or PPO), and more than 60 percent of those polled favored

tougher government regulation of managed care programs even if it raised their healthcare costs. In a 1998 *Newsweek* poll, 81 percent felt that protecting patients' rights in HMOs was the top domestic priority for Congress, more important than education, social security, or tax issues.

In a Harris poll taken the same year, more than 50 percent felt that health insurance companies were doing a bad job in serving their customers. A follow-up Harris poll (in 2003) showed that 57 percent of Americans wanted the government to have greater regulatory control over managed care companies and health insurance companies in general. The poll also showed that only 7 percent thought that health insurance companies were "generally honest and trustworthy." This is in line with a general trend that shows that consumers want regulations to be tightened on big business across the board.

A Gallup/CNN/*USA Today* poll in 1998 noted that "public furor against managed care is so intense that the idea of establishing certain patient's rights in the new managed care environment has become one of the hottest issues in the '98 elections."

A Kaiser Family Foundation survey in 2001 found that 81 percent of consumers supported a Patients' Bill of Rights. (When told that health insurance premiums might rise by about $20 per month for a typical family, support for a federal Patients' Bill of Rights fell from 81 percent to 58 percent.) Seventy-five percent said that healthcare issues should be very important priorities for the president and Congress, and 50 percent of the consumers said they would not consider it a real Patients' Bill of Rights without the right to sue their HMO (although 80 percent of the consumers would be willing to accept limits on lawsuit damages).[10]

The Impact of Sicko

In June 2007, documentary filmmaker Michael Moore's movie *Sicko* received International acclaim at the Cannes Film Festival. It also received widespread distribution and achieved the second highest opening weekend grosses for a documentary, after Moore's *Fahrenheit 9/11*. Critics, conservative and liberal alike, hailed it as a well-researched exposé of the healthcare situation in the United States.[11] It also generated criticism and controversy.[12] As of August 2007, *Sicko* had grossed more than $23 million, making it one of the largest grossing documentaries.

Most important, *Sicko* drew attention to the problems with the for-profit health insurance and pharmaceutical industry. Moore did not dwell on the issue of the 47 million Americans who have no healthcare insurance, which, he said, was a separate issue that needed immediate attention from Congress. He focused on those who actually have insurance and how they are affected by the current state of the industry. He pointed out that:

- The United States is the only industrialized nation that does not provide universal healthcare to its citizens.

- According to the World Health Organization, the United States is number 37 in the world when it comes to healthcare—just behind Costa Rica, at number 36, and just ahead of Slovenia, at number 38.

- In the United States, healthcare costs run nearly $7,000 per person, while in Cuba, it is around $251 per person. Nevertheless, Cuba has a lower infant mortality rate and a longer average life span than the United States.

- The suspected terrorist detainees being held at the U.S. military facility at Guantanamo receive round-the-clock universal healthcare, including dental, vision, and diagnostic tests, paid for by U.S. taxpayers. Yet, three Ground Zero rescue workers suffering from 9/11 injuries had been unable to get expensive medical treatment from any insurance plan. Moore brought them to Cuba in a small boat to make a point: trying to seek the same medical attention for these heroes, which is given to the detainee suspects at Guantánamo. The rescue workers apparently fell between the cracks, because they were volunteers, did not have their own health insurance, and were not on a city or state government health plan. They received healthcare, from the Cuban medical system.

▪ About 30 percent of the private healthcare industry's costs go toward administration. Medicare, a U.S. government entity that gets consistently high marks from consumers, spends about 1 percent on administration.

▪ The single-payer system of universal healthcare (everyone is eligible, the government pays) as practiced in Canada, the United Kingdom, and France is extremely well received by their citizens. While the wait times for specialists may be long in nonemergency situations (four weeks), those Moore interviewed felt that care was good and without financial burden. Life spans in all three countries are longer than in the United States.

Following the movie's release, the Kaiser Family Foundation conducted a poll to determine the impact of *Sicko*.[13] The level of interest was surprising. A large portion of the group polled (46 percent) had seen, heard, or read something about the movie. Forty-five percent of those polled said that they had discussions with friends, co-workers, or family members about the U.S. health system as a result of the movie, and 43 percent said that because of the movie, they were more likely to think there is a need to reform the healthcare system. Thirty-seven percent were more likely to think that other countries had a better approach to healthcare, and 27 percent said they were paying more attention to the positions of presidential candidates on healthcare in the 2008 election.

The other surprise was that this issue crossed party lines, and while Democrats generally were more in favor of universal health-care than Republicans, nevertheless, Republicans showed strong interest. That is a significant finding, and it means the public is aware of this issue. Finally, the Kaiser poll found that a majority of those polled (51 percent) viewed health insurers unfavorably, and HMOs were viewed unfavorably by almost half of those polled (46 percent).

INSURANCE IN THE MOVIES

Motion pictures, which usually reflect the sign and pulse of the times, have been openly critical of healthcare insurance in particular and the insurance industry in general. Movies have portrayed the insurance industry as intentionally delaying and denying legitimate claims and/or taking the occasional big hit in a damage award in court as a cost of doing business.

The Rainmaker (1997), based on the novel by John Grisham, dramatically portrayed a ruthless insurance company chief executive (Jon Voight) "playing the percentages" when it came to lawsuits. This involved the practice of "delaying and denying" legitimate claims, hoping that claimants do not have the stamina, legal resources, or money to sue the insurance company. If the company "gets hit," loses an occasional case, and has to pay, that is just part of the "cost of doing business."

In *As Good as It Gets* (1997), an arrogant HMO limits the care of the ailing child of a hardworking waitress. When I saw the film, the audience applauded when the waitress (Helen Hunt) bitterly denounces the tactics of the HMO.

In the 2002 film *John Q* (2002), the healthcare insurance issue took on more urgency when an insurance company refuses to pay for a life-saving operation for a young boy. The desperate father (Denzel Washington) grabs a weapon and commandeers a hospital, holding everyone hostage until doctors agree to do the procedure.

The McKinsey Report: A Big Surprise

In August 2007, the public uproar reached a crescendo when a report crossed the news wires concerning the insurance industry's claims processing procedure. Both *Bloomberg Markets Magazine* and *NOW*, PBS's investigative news show, recently uncovered a confidential report written by McKinsey & Company (a privately held New York–based consulting firm with more than 14,000 employees in forty countries) advising insurance companies on how to increase profits by streamlining claims handling.[14] State Farm and Allstate, the top two insurers in the homeowners insurance category, were alleged to be recipients of this advice.

According to documents obtained in a court case, including McKinsey's PowerPoint slides, the company advised insurers to "Sit and Wait."[15] One slide featured an alligator with that very caption. McKinsey's explanation of the slide was that delaying settlements and stalling court proceedings was a tactic the insurer could use to discourage claimants; that is, the insurer might wear claimants down to the point where they dropped a challenge. Even if the tactic did not succeed, the insurer would be retaining the money longer, thereby making more on its investments.

Another PowerPoint slide, for Allstate, read "Good Hands or Boxing Gloves." McKinsey's explanation for this slide was that if a claimant accepts a lowball settlement, Allstate should treat the person with "Good Hands," the company's advertising motto. If, on the other hand, the policyholder protests or hires a lawyer, Allstate should put on the "Boxing Gloves" and fight back. In a third slide, entitled "Zero-Sum Economic Game," insurers were reminded that there are winners and losers, and the insurer can win by paying out no more than it has to, so it can keep more of its premium income.

Insurers fought to keep the McKinsey report under seal and unavailable to the public. However, because of the *Bloomberg Markets Magazine* article, the *NOW* television report, and the fact that several courts ordered the materials produced, the report is now out in the open and raising more than eyebrows.

The Bloomberg magazine article and the PBS television report stated that Allstate raised its net income from 1996 to 2006 by 140 percent simply by paying out less in claims to customers (79 percent of premium income paid out in claims in 1996, versus 58 percent of premium income paid out in claims in 2006). Allstate also earned $2.08 billion in profits in 1996, versus $4.99 billion in 2006.

The *Bloomberg* article stated:

> Paying out less to victims of catastrophes has helped produce record profits. In the past 12 years, insurance company net income has soared—even in the wake of Hurricane Katrina, the worst natural disaster in U.S. history. Property-casualty insurers, which cover damage to homes and cars, reported their highest-ever profit of $73 billion last year, up 49 percent from $49 billion in 2005, according to Highline Data LLC, a Cambridge, Massachusetts–based firm that compiles insurance industry data.[16]

State Farm has issued a strong denial of the Bloomberg and *NOW* stories, citing what it considers many inaccuracies and distortions.[17] The Insurance Information Institute, the trade information arm of the industry, took issue with the story's tone and errors in math.[18] As of this writing, neither Allstate nor any other insurer except State Farm has responded to the stories; more important, as of this writing, neither Bloomberg nor PBS has retracted any part of their stories.

The Need for Mental Health Insurance Parity

Mental health parity—providing the same insurance coverage for mental health treatment as that offered for medical and surgical treatment—or the lack of it is another concern bothering consumers. As of January 2007, thirty-eight states had enacted some form of mental health parity law. Twelve had not—and there was no national standard.

Mental health parity as part of proper HMO and other health insurance benefits came to the attention of the public through the widely televised case of Texas resident Andrea Yates, who was convicted of drowning her five children in a bathtub, one by one. It seemed clear to many people that Yates was mentally ill when she caused the deaths of the children, and thus should not have been convicted of murder. However, Texas law severely restricts the defendant's ability to plead a mental illness defense. (Her conviction was later overturned by an appellate court because of problems with expert testimony in the case, not on the issue of Texas law's definition of mental illness.)

It is not clear why the mother was not given proper medical attention for her known mental condition: post-partum depression and psychosis. Her husband, Russell "Rusty" Yates, claimed he tried to get proper psychiatric care for his wife, but—as he told TV anchor Katie Couric—"we couldn't get it."[19] The case greatly increased the awareness of the mental insurance issue.

In addition to limited coverage, claimants with mental illness sometimes face significant hurdles when it comes to collecting on the insurance they have. They may need to undergo independent medical examinations, which sometimes result in wildly different subjective opinions about the extent of their illness. In addition, many policy terms, such as what is "medically necessary" and "appropriate care," are ambiguous, undefined, or ill defined, and can cause unnecessary delay, termination of claim payment, or denial of the claim. If regulators do not periodically scrutinize insurance companies' claims payment practices, and the insurer embarks on a path of claim denial, lengthy litigation will most likely ensue, taking its emotional and economic toll on the waiting claimants.

Numerous mental health groups and others have been pushing the respective state legislatures and the federal government to adopt strong mental health benefit policies that will equalize mental and physical claim payments. Many states have some form of mental health parity, while others have no mental health parity provisions at all.

One of the strongest voices for the recognition of fair mental health benefits in insurance health policies grew out of an exhaustive 500-page report by an expert panel, headed by former U.S. Surgeon General David Satcher. The report, released in December 2000, concluded that mental disorders are legitimate illnesses that respond to specific treatments, just as other health conditions respond to medical interventions. It further stated that society could no longer afford to view mental health as separate and unequal to general health issues.[20]

Significantly, national mental health parity received a political endorsement when President George W. Bush, on April 29, 2002, called for legislation to eliminate disparities between the coverage of patients with mental and physical ailments. Speaking at a job training facility for people recovering from mental illness, in Albuquerque, New Mexico, Bush clearly supported the idea of mental health parity. He stated, "Our health insurance system must treat mental illness like any other disease." He said that he did not believe that mental health parity legislation would significantly increase the cost of healthcare.

While the president did not endorse a specific bill or detail provisions he would support, he signaled that he would favor wider insurance coverage for the most serious mental illnesses, including major depression, bipolar disorder, schizophrenia, and obsessive-compulsive disorder. Opposition to Bush's endorsement came from certain lawmakers, as well as some in the insurance industry and small business community, who feared the higher costs that might be imposed on employers.

In 2003, several senators—most notably Gordon Smith (R, Washington)—urged increased federal funding for treatment to help stop teen suicides. The legislation proposed by Smith passed, authorizing $82 million over three years for youth suicide prevention programs.[21] After he spoke out, several other leading lawmakers recommended that Congress look at mental health as a serious national problem.

Since the McCarran-Ferguson Act mandates that each state controls and regulates insurance within its borders, physical and mental health insurance benefits can be (and are) quite different from state to state. A very positive result of the passage of federal mental health parity legislation would be that states that already have adopted some form of mental health parity, together with those states that have not adopted any form of parity, would be required to have a uniform federal standard. States could add on to this standard if they wish.

Katrina Redux

At the end of 2007, we were reminded again of the societal anger that still is Katrina. When Katrina is discussed in Louisiana, the insurance companies are regarded as "a new villain in the tales people tell about the slow recovery." Reports have come out of the Gold Coast states that insurance companies have offered only sparse amounts in the remaining settlements and have "dribbled out payments, deliberately underestimated the costs of repairs, dropped longtime customers and sharply increased the price of coverage."[22] More than 6,000 insurance lawsuits were filed in federal district court in Louisiana. As of the end of 2007, more than half of them, amounting to millions of dollars in claims, were still pending without resolution. Some of the cases were referred to state courts. The Louisiana Department of Insurance was swamped with formal complaints, more than 4,700 in 2006 alone.

The public uproar reflects a real, palpable awakening about many issues and a major case of distrust of the industry. Polls critical of the industry and motion pictures expressing anger point to significant issues, such as stacked-deck legislatures, HMO problems, the need for a Patients' Bill of Rights, lack of proper mental health coverage, and confusion over long-term care. Recent revelations in documentaries such as *Sicko* show a broken healthcare system and other countries with a well-functioning universal healthcare system. Investigations and the media alert the public to broker bid rigging, fraud, biased experts, systematic patterns of claims denial, rogue executives, overpricing, questionable market conduct—and billions of dollars of Katrina claims still unpaid. This makes for an unhappy public. Since 2008 is a presidential election year, it was likely the problems in the insurance industry would transform the public uproar and distrust into concrete, positive proposals for the country.

What will consumers see and do if there is no change? What they will see are increased premium costs, diminished benefits, claims disputes, and nonuniform regulations. They are and will not be happy about it.

What will they do? Let's put it this way: Would you continue to put money in a bank or brokerage firm in which you fail to trust the bankers or brokers? Would you continue to put money into insurance companies in which you fail to trust the executives? Probably not. Could we be heading toward a national consumer boycott of insurance? If only one in ten policyholders suddenly decided not to purchase insurance, the 10 percent drop in insurance premium income could cause a seismic collapse in the insurance industry. If the insurance industry takes in more than $1 trillion per year, as it does, and it has a 10 percent drop in revenue ($100 billion per year), it could push insurance carriers into an economic stone wall. To stay in business and operate profitably, they might raise premiums (for those who still wanted or needed to buy insurance) and/or reduce benefits, increase deductibles, and probably fight every close claim in court. That would create tremendous market resistance, unstable insurers, and a collapse of the system. We do not need that scenario.

Notes

1. Ruby Bailey, "Vigilance On Capitol Hill—Dingell Steps Up for Patients Father's Fight Drives Congressman's Battle For More Rights," *Detroit Free Press*, July 26, 2001, Thursday Metro Final Edition, Section: Nws, p. 1a.

2. I had the opportunity to testify before a congressional committee in which Representative Dingell was the questioner. He was a quick study and very perceptive, arriving at the core issues expeditiously, after which he and his staff set out to thoroughly research those of particular note.

3. "Voters' Anger at HMOs Plays as Hot Political Issue," *New York Times*, May 17, 1998.

4. "Employer Health Benefits 2006 Annual Survey," Kaiser Family Foundation and Health Research and Educational Trust, September 2006.

5. "Consumer Expenditures in 2005," U.S. Department of Labor, U.S. Bureau of Labor Statistics, Report 998, February 2007.

6. United States Census Bureau, August 29, 2006.

7. CBS News/*New York Times* poll, January 20–25, 2006.

8. Gallup Poll, November 9–12, 2006.

9. CNN/Opinion Research Corporation Poll, May 4–6, 2007.

10. *Washington Post*/ABC Poll, July 12, 1998; *Newsweek* Poll, November 5–8, 1998, conducted by Princeton Survey Research Associates; Harris Poll, March 11–16, 1998; CBS News/*NY Times* Poll, June 7–9, 1998; Gallup/CNN/*USA Today* Poll, April 17–19, 1998; Kaiser Family Foundation Survey, August 30, 2001.

11. See, for example, Alissa Simon, May 19, 2007; Roger Friedman, Fox News, May 20, 2007.

12. See, for example, David Denby, "Do No Harm," *New Yorker*, July 2, 2007; Michael Moynihan, "Michael Moore's Shticko," *Reason Magazine*, June 22, 2007.

13. Kaiser Family Foundation, Kaiser Health Tracking Survey: Election 2008, August 2–8, 2007.

14. David Dietz and Darrell Preston, "The Insurance Hoax—Property Insurers Use Secret Tactics to Cheat Customers Out of Payments—As Profits Break Records," *Bloomberg Markets Magazine*, September 2007; see also David Brancaccio, "Home Insurance 9-1-1," *NOW*, PBS-TV, August 17, 2007.

15. The McKinsey report was viewed briefly at a May 2005 hearing in Fayette Circuit Court, Lexington, Kentucky, in a 1997 auto accident case, *Geneva Hager v. Allstate*. Judge Thomas Clark allowed the viewing, but sealed the records before and after the hearing.

16. Dietz and Preston, "The Insurance Hoax."

17. For State Farm's response to the *Bloomberg Markets Magazine* article, see http://www.statefarm.com/about/media/bloomberg.asp.

18. For the response of Robert P. Hartwig, president of the Insurance Information Institute, to the *Bloomberg Markets Magazine* article, see http://www.state farm.com/about/media/bloomberg_letter.asp.

19. Rusty Yates appeared on "Today," NBC-TV's network morning talk show, interviewed by host Katie Couric shortly after Ms. Yates' conviction in June 2001. As to his comment about proper psychiatric care for his wife and that "we couldn't get it," it is generally believed that he was referring to the fact that while his wife had undergone treatment by a psychiatrist and with medication, he believed that the advice by the psychiatrist and the meds prescribed, were wrong, and there were insurance limitations preventing proper treatment. For example, Rusty Yates claimed that the psychiatrist refused to hospitalize Mrs. Yates, took her off the antipsychotic drug Haldol, and two weeks later, when the drug had worn off, her five children were drowned.

20. David Satcher, "Mental Health: A Report of the Surgeon General" (Washington, D.C.: Government Printing Office, December 2000).

21. On September 9, 2003, Congress passed the Garrett Lee Smith Memorial Act (S2634).

22. Leslie Eaton and Joseph B. Treaster, "Insurers Bear Brunt of Anger in New Orleans," *New York Times*, September 3, 2007.

THE SOLUTION

The U.S. Congress ponders the insurance crisis.
Cartoon by Marshall Ramsey. Reprinted with permission of Copley News Service.

CHAPTER 8

Fifty Nonuniform State Fiefdoms

"They [the 50 state insurance commissioners] are like snowflakes, it's rare to find any two alike."

    —Brian Atchinson, Executive Director, Insurance Marketplace Standards Association, July 8, 2003

"I think we could do a better job of consumer outreach, to involve consumer interests in what we do."

    —Joel Ario, acting Pennsylvania Insurance Commissioner, September 20, 2007

The issues in the insurance industry are alarming, and one must ask the following questions: Why are problems occurring with greater severity and frequency than ever before? Why are the states saddled with the Herculean task of individually correcting the problems of a nationwide insurance industry? Why doesn't the federal government have oversight and control over the industry?

The Root of the Problem
The McCarran-Ferguson Act

To find a cure for the many issues confronting the insurance industry, one must first determine the causes of the problems, which, in turn, would lead to the weakest link of the chain. Most people are surprised to learn that—unlike most areas of daily life, where the federal government exerts considerable regulatory power and oversight—there is virtually no federal agency that oversees or regulates the insurance industry. In every other major industry that affects us every day, the federal government has ultimate control—in agriculture, banking, commerce, communication, defense, education, energy, environment, food and drug, health and human services, homeland security, housing, labor, national security, securities, transportation, and the like—but not in the insurance arena. The reason for that lies in the McCarran-Ferguson Act of 1945. Since its passage more than half a century ago, the federal government has tied its own hands and has yet to untie them.

The antiquated McCarran-Ferguson Act gives almost blanket antitrust immunity to insurance companies.[1] Even more important, the act does not allow the federal government to get involved directly in regulating the "business of insurance," but leaves it to each state to regulate this vast complex industry and to fix the problems within its particular borders. As a key section of the act says, "The business of insurance, and every person engaged therein, shall be subject to the laws of the several States which relate to the regulation or taxation of such business. . . ."[2] Because the McCarran-Ferguson Act requires state regulation, it has spawned fifty separate state insurance fiefdoms, with varying budgets, nonuniform state laws, and a cumbersome regulatory maze, resulting in very spotty consumer protection.

However well the McCarran-Ferguson Act worked in the past, the insurance industry, in large part, has changed. Since the act was passed, the industry, sensing a vacuum in the state regulatory environment, has become more predatory and more concerned with shareholder needs than the needs of policyholders.

Because of the lack of federal regulation and oversight of the insurance industry, whether the insurer or the insured benefits in terms of pricing, administration, or proper claims handling rules depends on each state's regulatory environment. It need not be this way. The McCarran-Ferguson Act is not helping the insurance industry in today's fast-paced international business environment; in fact, the act harms insurer and consumer alike.

A Brief History of Insurance Regulation in the United States

In order to understand where we are today, it is important to understand how we arrived here. In the 1800s, insurance was considered a matter of state regulation. Although the U.S. Constitution's Commerce Clause (in Article I, Section 8) gives the federal government the power and authority to regulate business whose activities crossed state lines ("interstate commerce"), the insurance business operated locally, within each state's borders. Thus, each state was given the duty to regulate it.

This was confirmed in the 1868 case *Paul v. Virginia*, where a New York broker was convicted of violating a Virginia insurance licensing law. The U.S. Supreme Court upheld the use of Virginia law to convict an out-of-state broker because, it said, an insurance transaction was not commerce and therefore could not be considered interstate commerce; thus, the federal government was not permitted to regulate it. Numerous decisions conformed to that ruling until the case of *U.S. v. South-Eastern Underwriters Association*, decided by the U.S. Supreme Court in 1944.

In the South-Eastern Underwriters case, several insurance defendants were charged with federal price fixing and conspiracy to monopolize trade. The Supreme Court, recognizing the changes that had occurred in the industry, completely reversed itself and ruled that insurance indeed crosses state lines and affects people in numerous states and, therefore, must be deemed a federal issue, subject to federal law.[3]

The Court held that insurance rating bureaus, which were created to suggest insurance rates to insurers, were involved in interstate commerce; therefore, they were subject to the federal antitrust laws, and the federal government has jurisdiction over the industry. The South-Eastern Underwriters case immediately exposed the rating bureaus and the insurers to be subject to federal antitrust price-fixing charges, which carry civil and criminal penalties. The decision caught many in the industry and state regulators off guard and sent them reeling.

In one stroke of the judicial pen, the Supreme Court's ruling threatened to make the National Association of Insurance Commissioners (NAIC) and the state-by-state regulatory system obsolete. Insurance would now be considered interstate commerce and, therefore, rating bureaus or other agencies meeting to discuss the pricing of insurance or other competitive matters would be subject to federal antitrust law. This caused widespread panic among those who had built up a political and bureaucratic system based on the principle of state regulation. After more than seventy-five years of state regulation of the insurance industry, federal regulation and federal intervention was now on the insurance industry's doorstep.

In 1945, reacting to the South-Eastern Underwriters case and enormous political lobbying by the industry against federal regulation, Congress was pushed to pass the McCarran-Ferguson Act, which put regulation squarely back in the hands of each state. The act, rushed through and approved in Congress in nine months, had the effect of reversing the Supreme Court's South-Eastern Underwriters ruling. Thus, notwithstanding the Supreme Court ruling— which clearly determined that insurance is an interstate product and therefore should be federally regulated—Congress, by passing the McCarran-Ferguson Act, handed the power to regulate insurance back to the individual states.

At the time that the McCarran-Ferguson Act was enacted, although the business of insurance had some characteristics of interstate commerce, it was still predominantly local or statewide in character. This is no longer the case. The insurance product as it exists today is much more national, even international, in character than it was in 1945. Furthermore, it is huge in terms of the amount of money flowing through the system.

The State of State Regulation

In the year 2006, the insurance industry's premiums for all types of insurance policies sold in the United States amounted to more than $1.4 trillion—all regulated on a state-by-state basis. In the same year, there were 393,654 consumer complaints (more than 7,570 per week) filed with the insurance commissioners pursuant to the separate laws of the fifty states, the four territories (American Samoa, Guam, Puerto Rico, and the U.S. Virgin Islands), and the District of Columbia.

This massive number of consumer complaints does not include more than 2.5 million consumer inquiries (more than 48,000 per week) to insurance departments nationwide in 2006.[4] Nor does it include the thousands of formal lawsuits involving insurance claims that were filed in our court system across the country. NAIC publications indicate that the numbers of complaints have remained at more than 400,000 per year for the last several years prior to 2006. The NAIC was unable to determine how many complaints are resolved each year.[5]

Can our state regulatory system really handle this? Not as currently constituted.

A Question of Money

To administer, regulate, and enforce the insurance industry, the average state insurance department needs a strong and fully paid staff. Yet a state's insurance department budget is usually woefully small. The NAIC reports that nationwide, state insurance department budgets in 2006 were only .08 percent of the average premium collected. In other words, for every $100 of premium paid for an insurance policy, the amount the states have budgeted for the state insurance department regulation of the industry is an average of eight cents.

There is also a big disparity between the overall amount of tax revenue collected by each state as a percentage of premiums insurance companies collect in that state. The average tax revenue of all states was 1.19 percent of revenues as a percentage of premiums in 2006. However, since that figure varies by state, one state may receive only .63 percent of premiums for its coffers (Wisconsin), while another state may receive 2.97 percent of premiums—four times more—for its state tax revenues (New Mexico). The difference in tax revenues paid on premiums could mean the difference in how a state budgets its regulation of insurance for its citizens. Citizens of some states are protected; citizens of other states may not be.

Collection and Allocation Methods

Compounding the problem of inadequate budgets for the state insurance departments are the different methods of allocating taxes used in the various states. Some have "dedicated funding" of tax revenues received on insurance premiums, which means that almost every dollar collected by taxing insurance premiums goes to administer insurance regulations. Most states have "general funding," meaning that the insurance premium taxes collected go into a general fund for the entire state, and the state's budget for the insurance department comes from that general fund. Some have a "blended funding" mechanism, which is a combination of methods of raising funds for the state.[6]

Interestingly, of the more than $16 billion in state insurance tax revenue collected nationwide in 2006, only an average of 7.11 percent actually went to fund state insurance departments. The rest goes to other parts of state government. Some state insurance departments do retain 100 percent of the insurance tax revenue (Michigan) for the state insurance department; in other states, the insurance department can retain only 2.35 percent, the rest going into the general state fund (Georgia). Obviously, in a stronger consumer-active insurance state, there is more pressure to spend more heavily on insurance department regulatory staff.

It is clear from this analysis that many states rely on insurance tax dollars to fund other state projects, unrelated to consumer insurance protection. This can mean that they fail to use enough of the insurance tax revenue to fund an adequate state insurance department budget, which may seriously affect the way in which insurance products are delivered in the state.

This revenue can be a huge windfall to the state, and states jealously guard the insurance tax revenue to fund their non-insurance–related projects. For example, Indiana was cited years ago for attracting insurance carriers presumably because the insurance department had weak budgets, and therefore, a weak regulatory staff. In 2006, the Indiana Insurance Department budget as a percentage of revenue collected was still weak, only 4.21 percent. This was one of the lowest in the country (the average state budget is almost twice that amount, 7.11 percent of insurance premium tax revenue collected).[7] Indiana's budget as a percentage of premium collected was .03 percent, also low (the average state percentage of premium used for budgets is approximately .08 percent, more than two and a half times that of Indiana). These numbers indicate that Indiana's state government is using a large amount of its tax on insurance premium revenue for other state purposes and, relative to the amount of money collected, still has a small budget for its insurance department, which in turn may cause a weak regulatory climate.

State Insurance Commissioners

In some states, insurance regulation may be dictated by how the insurance commissioner is chosen. In most states, the governor appoints the insurance commissioner, who is confirmed by the state legislature; some states and territories allow the public to elect their commissioner. (See Figure 8-1.)

Some observers believe that an elected state insurance commissioner is more responsive to the needs of the electorate in general

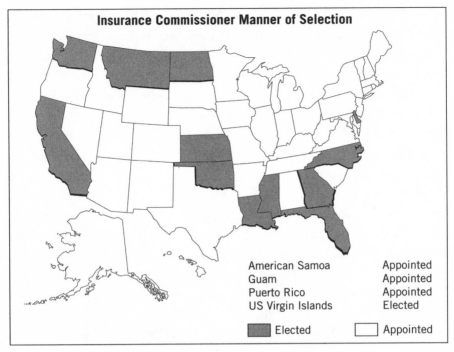

Figure 8-1. Method of selection of state insurance commissioners in the United States.
Source: Robert W. Klein, *A Regulator's Introduction to the Insurance Industry* (NAIC, 1999).
Reprinted with permission of the NAIC.

and the consumer in particular, because of the need to be reelected. Others believe that an appointed commissioner is devoid of political obligations, and that the governor will choose the most qualified person to do the very best for the citizens of that state.

In 2003, analysts studied the performance and results of regulatory bodies and concluded that direct election strengthens the power of voters. Using data on regulatory outcomes from the states, the analysts found that states with elected regulators are more pro-consumer in their regulatory policies.[8] The NAIC notes that different approaches to selection (elected versus appointed) cause the length of the commissioners' terms to vary from state to state. The duties of the commissioner also differ among states. In the majority of states, the insurance department is a separate agency. In other states, the commissioners' responsibilities overlap in other areas, such as holding the title of fire marshal, state auditor, or commissioner of securities.[9] Once again, the attention to detail in the insurance area depends on the state and the respective commissioner.

In December 2007, Bloomberg news reported on the turndown by insurance carriers of several expensive procedures (bone marrow transplant and chemotherapy cancer treatment claims); and state insurance departments agreeing with the insurance carrier, after the claimants had appealed to the departments to intercede on their behalf. The in-depth article studied the role of state insurance department regulators, and discovered the extremely close nature of many state insurance department regulators to the industry they are supposed to regulate; oft-times resulting in weak protection, or no protection, for the consumer.[10]

The Bloomberg reporters cited, for example, a number of insurance regulators who were accused of corrupt practices such as embezzlement, taking bribes, or lying to the FBI. The article also focused on conflict of interest charges including contributions to regulators from insurance companies and having expensive trips paid for by the industry, as well as the issues of a revolving door policy.

The problems are not new, but have continued unchecked. As early as 1979, the GAO, Congress's investigative arm, cautioned about a "revolving door" for insurance regulators.[11] Over the past two decades, 50 percent of the insurance commissioners, 74 of 180 regulators, came from or went into major insurance industry jobs, blurring the distinction between government and industry.[12] In April of 2007, CFA Insurance Director J. Robert Hunter testified before Congress on the subject of state regulation. He expressed serious concern over the fact that five of the last six presidents of NAIC now work as lobbyists for insurance companies or directly for the insurance industry they are supposed to regulate. Hunter told Congress that part of the reason that the states are not effective as regulators was this revolving door between industry and the insurance commissions.[13]

Industry spokesmen have argued that many of the accusations were unjustified, and that it was unfair to paint all insurance regulators with the same brush. They stated that insurers and regulators comply with state insurance laws.

The bottom line from this writer's standpoint, is that the article demonstrated a glaring problem with the current insurance system, which needs to be addressed.

The Impact of McCarran-Ferguson

The McCarran-Ferguson Act has been roundly criticized by the media and others for allowing the states to create a climate in which the deck is stacked in favor of the insurance industry, and against the consumer. The General Accounting Office identified this as a problem in its 1979 report, and it has remained a problem to this day.[14] By requiring the states to enact individual insurance laws, the act moved away from a uniform standard that federal regulation would have mandated. Instead, fifty laws were created, tenuously held together by the NAIC, a body without statutory authority or enforcement power.

The impact of McCarran-Ferguson takes many forms, including:

- The packing of legislative insurance committees with insurance industry–affiliated lawmakers, thereby controlling insurance legislation

- The appointment of state insurance commissioners who are heavily pro-industry

- The application of subtle political pressure to keep the consumer uninformed

- Underfunding and understaffing of the state insurance departments

- The failure to encourage a strong audit, investigative, and enforcement arm

In Pennsylvania, disclosure statements showed that nearly10 percent of the 253 legislators who served in the session that ended December 1998 had direct ties to the insurance industry. Some were insurance agents, some owned insurance companies, and some were lawyers representing insurance companies.[15] The presence of legislators with ties to the industry continues today.[16] In addition, as previously stated, McCarran-Ferguson exempts the insurance industry from federal antitrust laws and fosters a climate favorable to the growth of a patchwork of legislation and regulation among the states. Each state has its own licensing requirements for companies, agents, and brokers; each state sets its own rate- and policy form–filing requirements; and each state sets its own rules as to what information the consumer must be given.[17]

The complaint process in each state can be quite different. This is not only a problem for the consumer complainant. Compliance with fifty different regulatory schemes can be costly, time consuming, and an administrative, political, and legal nightmare for insurers, brokers, and agents as well.

Consumer advocates and consumer protection mechanisms vary widely among the states. One state may have a dedicated consumer advocate department to help resolve a consumer claim with a carrier, but most states have no such advocate. In fact, according to the NAIC, as of 2001, only twenty of the fifty states had a dedicated consumer advocate position specifically established to protect and enforce rights on behalf of consumers.[18] That leaves a staggering thirty states—or 60 percent—without a dedicated consumer advocate position. As of this writing, the number of consumer advocate positions has not increased.

While many states have some form of consumer complaint analyst, or say that they have an active consumer department, in practice, many have only a small bureau dealing with these issues. In many states, these departments do not have the clout of a consumer advocate officer or office, whose sole job is as a watchdog and enforcer of the rights of consumers under that state's law. Furthermore, none of the consumer advocates has subpoena or enforcement powers.[19]

Although there has been nearly a 100 percent increase in the aggregate budget for state insurance departments for the ten-year period ending in 2000 (from $439.3 million nationwide to more than $880 million), the creation of state consumer advocate positions has not kept pace with the need.

Notwithstanding the impact of legislators who are directly or indirectly in the employ of the insurance industry, some states are finding ways to circumvent the legislature and to create consumer advocate positions without legislation. Pennsylvania is one example. One of the largest states in which insurance is transacted, Pennsylvania currently has no legislatively created office of consumer advocate for insurance. Although there have been many attempts to create such an office legislatively, the bills failed. Pennsylvania has an insurance industry–heavy legislature, whose members are opposed to a designated consumer advocate.

Commendably, in January 2005, Governor Edward G. Rendell and Pennsylvania Insurance Commissioner Diane Koken found a way administratively to create a new Office of Insurance Consumer Liaison, which is similar to an office of consumer advocate within the insurance department. Since its inception the group has been soliciting input from consumers and working with insurers to create a fair playing field. As with most other consumer advocate positions, the Office of Insurance Consumer Liaison has no enforcement power.[20]

State regulations pertaining to solvency of insurers are very uneven. Some states examine an insurer's financial condition thoroughly. They look at a company's claims-paying ability and balance sheet very carefully before allowing it to start or to continue doing business in the state, and they insist on properly held reserves (amounts that are set aside to pay potential claims). Other states, either because they are less thorough or are understaffed, accept an internal insurance company auditor's certification of the adequacy and strength of a company's reserves. They fail to apply truly independent audit methods to verify the amount of reserves, and they do not verify whether the reserves physically exist, other than on paper.[21]

State guaranty funds (the pool paid out in the event of an admitted insurer's default) are different depending on the state. Generally, the state fund provides a limited maximum payout of between $100,000 and $300,000 per claim; therefore, if a claim is large, the "guarantees" are limited to the maximum allowed. In addition, if the claims against the insolvent company are complicated and involve other stakeholders and several states, the litigation may take years.

The Impact of Nonuniformity of State Laws on Consumers

The lack of uniform laws among the states directly hurts the consumer in a variety of ways. Among them are "bad faith" damages and "notice of claim" provisions in the insurance policy, as well as transportation and medical malpractice insurance issues.

Bad Faith Claims

In addition to the underlying claim for breach of contract, the bad faith cause of action allows an aggrieved insured to sue the insurance carrier for reckless claims handling in a separate lawsuit, allowing the judge or jury to award punitive damages, if warranted. It is a powerful weapon for consumers, and it is feared by insurers since bad faith damages can include attorney fees, interest and costs, and unlimited punitive damages.

Not all states permit bad faith lawsuits, and the rules governing them vary significantly from state to state.[22] Even if you live in a state that allows bad faith lawsuits, you must carefully check each jurisdiction to determine what you must prove in court—the so-called burden of proof requirements, which are much more stringent in some states than others.

Where bad faith lawsuits are allowed, bad faith damages are an important part of the legal and financial landscape. Initiation of a first party (for example, a homeowner, disability, life, or health claimant) bad faith claim against an insurer brings the nonuniformity problem into sharp focus. Bad faith laws tend to level the playing field between the claimant and the carrier, who is exposed to the possibility of a multimillion-dollar punitive damage award for reckless claims handling. The catch is that it depends on which state has jurisdiction.

Punitive damage awards against insurance carriers can be huge and are growing larger, so it is no wonder that insurers do not like to operate in states that offer such a remedy. Between 1968 and 1971, there were ninety-one punitive damage awards, totaling $6,994,000 in the states of California, Texas, New York, Illinois, and Florida. Twenty years later, there were 433 punitive damage awards in those states totaling $790,247,000—a 100-fold increase.[23]

Late Notice of Claim

"Late notice of claim," or "late claim notice," is an innocuous enough looking requirement in an insurance policy, but it can become a major problem in some states. In some states, if you do not file your claim within the time specified in the insurance policy, the insurer can claim prejudice (saying that because you filed late, the insurer did not have enough time to check facts or interview witnesses, or, where applicable, evidence may no longer exist or may have disappeared to their prejudice). State rulings on late notice vary widely and can have a very dramatic effect on a claim.[24] In some jurisdictions, the carrier is not required to show prejudice; in others, prejudice is presumed and is a serious factor. In some places, prejudice is presumed but the policyholder can rebut the presumption; in still others, prejudice must be shown in some instances, but not in others, and in one state, actual and substantial prejudice must be shown by the carrier. In addition, the claim filing period varies from state to state. In some states, a policy can require that a notice of claim be filed in as short a period as thirty days, while in other states, a policy claim may be filed in as long as one or two years.

The claim filing period should be the same in every state (say, one year from the date of incident, unless there are special circumstances), which would make it easier for the policyholder to understand and comply. As matters stand, depending on the state of residence, a consumer risks not being paid because of late filing.

Other Nonuniformity Issues Affecting Consumers

In some states, certain types of insurance, such as comprehensive general liability insurance for freight railroads, is entirely exempt from state (and federal) regulation—which means the railroad is expected but not required to have insurance, leaving gaps in regulation and insurance coverage. For example, a claimant in a railroad crossing accident may find that the railroad is uninsured or underinsured, depending on the state.

In the area of medical malpractice insurance, states may require different malpractice insurance limits for physicians who are licensed to practice in that state. In addition, state government involvement in malpractice insurance pools also varies from state to state. Some states, like Pennsylvania, require that doctors carry a minimum of $1 million in professional liability insurance in order to maintain a license. The private insurance companies provide the first $500,000, and the government takes the second layer of $500,000. Pennsylvania also has an insurance pool for doctors who are unable to obtain coverage through private insurers for the first layer. Other states require less liability insurance and do not get involved directly with a layer of insurance. Uniformity would eliminate insurance as a reason for a physician to avoid practicing medicine in any state.

The Impact of Nonuniformity on Insurers

Similarly, insurers are battered by continual revision to the fifty state insurance laws. Each legislative body is different, with fifty different insurance commissioners. The different laws require constant review by an army of compliance attorneys and staff, as well as extra costs for filing of rate and policy approval forms and other specific state regulatory filings. Attention must also be paid to the licensing requirements, audits, local legal counsels, and lobbyists for each state.

As these examples illustrate, insurers who are subject to multiple state laws or relocate from one state to another may confront real and different problems. Whether it be life and health policies, or property and casualty policies, insurers will save millions if the system is standardized, creating uniformity and predictability.

Notes

1. The McCarran-Ferguson Act U.S. Code Title 15, Chapter 20, 15 U.S.C. section 1011 et seq, requires each state to regulate the "business of insurance" within

its borders, and exempts the insurers from the anti-trust regulations of the Sherman Act (price fixing, 1890), the Clayton Act (interlocking directorates, 1914), the Federal Trade Commission Act (deceptive practices in commerce, 1914), the Merchant Marine Act (antitrust laws, 1920), the National Labor Relations Act (labor disputes, 1935), and the Fair Labor Standards Act (employer-employee relations, 1938), to the extent that the relations are regulated by state law.

2. Ibid.

3. *U.S. v. South-Eastern Underwriters*, 322 U.S. 533 (1944), June 5, 1944. The U.S. Supreme Court's decision overturned judicial decisions spanning seventy-five years beginning with *Paul v. Virginia*, 8 Wall. 168 (1868).

4. NAIC, "2006 Insurance Department Resources Report" (Kansas City, Missouri: National Association of Insurance Commissioners, 2007).

5. Interview conducted with Laura Deatrick, the research analyst responsible for the NAIC Insurance Department Resources Report, June 2004.

6. NAIC, "2006 Insurance Department Resources Report."

7. Ibid.

8. Timothy Besley and Stephen Coate, "Elected Versus Appointed Regulators: Theory and Evidence," *Journal of the European Economic Association*, vol. 1, no. 5, September 2003, pp. 1176–1200.

9. NAIC, "2006 Insurance Department Resources Report."

10. David Dietz, Gary Cohn, and Darrell Preston, "Bribed Regulators Deceiving FBI Roil U.S. Insurance Customers," Bloomberg.com, December 27, 2007, accessible at http://www.bloomberg.com/apps/news?pid = 20601109&sid = aZ6fBu_fvkBc&refer = home.

    The claimants from New Mexico and Connecticut told Bloomberg news that they felt that the claim process had taken its emotional toll; they felt betrayed and powerless; and that the respective state insurance regulators let them down. The claimant from New Mexico ultimately received payment for the procedure—not from the insurance company—but from anonymous donors. The claimant from Connecticut finally succeeded in his claim, and received $250,000 from the insurance company for the procedure—but only after powerful people interceded (for example, Connecticut Attorney General Richard Blumenthal wrote the state insurance commissioner and suggested an investigation should be undertaken).

    The reporters concluded that the claimant, regulator, and insurer stories cited in the article are ". . . symptomatic of a fragmented system of regulation, created 150 years ago, that gives each state the power to regulate insurance companies."

11. See endnote in Chapter 5, GAO discussion in 1979 of "revolving door" policy for insurance regulators.

12. Dietz, Cohn, and Preston.

13. J. Robert Hunter, Insurance Director, Consumer Federation of America, Statement before Committee on Commerce, Science and Transportation, U.S. Senate, April 11, 2007.

14. See General Accounting Office Report to Congress, "Issues and Needed Improvements in State Regulation of the Insurance Business," 1979.

15. B. J. Phillips and Ken Dilanian, "Key Pa. Lawmakers Have Direct Ties to Insurance Industry," *Philadelphia Inquirer*, February 26, 1999.

16. Ibid.

17. See, for example, "Center Identifies Potential for Conflict in State Legislature," September 24, 2004, Center for Public Integrity, Washington, D.C. (Investigative Journalism in the Public Interest), which reported that of the 245 legislators in office in Pennsylvania in 2001, 21.2 percent sat on a legislative committee with authority over a profession or business in which they earned an income.

18. NAIC, "2006 Insurance Department Resources Report."

19. NAIC, "Insurance Department Resources Report 2001" (2002). Twenty states claimed to have salaried dedicated consumer advocate positions: Alaska, California, Florida, Iowa, Kansas, Kentucky, Louisiana, Maine, Maryland, Minnesota, Nebraska, New Hampshire, New Jersey, New Mexico, North Dakota, Ohio, Oregon, Virginia, Washington, and West Virginia. According to the NAIC's latest report, this number has not increased. (In 1994, only twelve states reported having a consumer advocate position.)

20. I was pleased to see the creation of the new Office of Insurance Consumer Liaison because, prior to the office's creation, I had submitted several position papers to both the governor and the insurance commissioner on the need for an Office of Consumer Advocate. In 2007, a new bill (House Bill 1121) to create a consumer advocate in Pennsylvania was introduced; the climate may now be right for the bill to pass, since voters appear to be focused on insurance issues. Hearings are being held but as of late 2007 the act has not referred out of committee for a vote.

21. On occasion, a serious dispute arises between an insurer's internal auditors, who may insist on a cautious approach to reserves for the payment of claims (which appear as a liability on the company's balance sheet), and top executives, who may desire a less conservative approach (which has the effect of making the company's balance sheet look better than it is).

22. For an expansive and excellent treatise on bad faith, see Stephen S. Ashley, *Bad Faith Actions, Liability and Damages*, 2nd ed. (West Publishing Group, 1997, as updated), in particular Chapter 9, which confirmed the "patchwork"

quilt of nonuniform bad faith law among the various jurisdictions in the United States. This patchwork of insurance laws on bad faith still exists today.

23. Peter Kinzler, *Journal of Insurance Regulation*, Spring 1997, vol. 15, no. 3.

24. See Laura A. Foggan, "An Insurer Perspective: Why Notice Is a Critical Element of Insurance Contracts" (Washington, D.C.: Practicing Law Institute, 2004). Foggan's excellent treatise on notice of claim points up the disparities among the state insurance laws.

Insurance industry being pulled in different directions.
Cartoon by Brad McMillan. Reprinted with permission of Cartoonstock.com.

CHAPTER 9

Winds of Change
How to Improve the Industry

"We must act on uniformity issues or the train will leave the station and we won't be driving it. . . . Our goal is not just reciprocity [between the states], it is uniformity.**"**

—Mike Pickens, then president of the NAIC, June 2003

Momentum for Change

In today's climate, many insurers and many in the public are urging a major rethinking of the industry. Others are going further and calling for the repeal or significant modification of the antiquated state regulatory system. For years, some insurance associations have been weighing in on the side of federal regulation. However, changes in the insurance industry usually take years, especially something like a sea change in the entire regulatory system.

At the National Association of Insurance Commissioners [NAIC] meeting in June 2003, I could sense change was in the air, as a steady stream of speakers took to the podium to raise the issue of changes that needed to be made to the state-regulated insurance industry. Among the big issues cited was the lack of uniformity of insurance laws between the states. Arkansas's Mike Pickens, who was then president of the NAIC, went on to admonish the assembled group, saying, "We [the NAIC] must act on uniformity issues or the train will leave the station and we won't be driving it. . . . Our goal is not just reciprocity [between the states], it is uniformity."

Senator Ben Nelson (D, Nebraska)—formerly director of the Nebraska Department of Insurance, chief of staff and executive vice president of the NAIC, and two-term Nebraska governor—warned the assembled body, "I'd suggest you [the NAIC] draft your own set of standards and set a timetable for true implementation. Otherwise, you'll be faced with reacting to the congressional process [new federal legislation]."

At an NAIC breakout subcommittee meeting, Jose Montemayor, the outspoken Texas insurance commissioner and chair of a number of important NAIC committees, voiced the opinion that the various state insurance filing requirements and state insurance regulations were a "hodgepodge," and he stressed that the NAIC "should have the goal of uniformity." He cited a few examples of the lack of uniformity: flat filing fees in some states, variable fees in others; name approval of new carriers in some states, not in others; fingerprinting of insurance producers (brokers or agents) in some states, not in others; as well as different interpretations of the same insurance regulations.

Representative Michael Oxley (R, Ohio)—a cosponsor of the then recently enacted Sarbanes-Oxley Act, which requires significantly more accountability of public company executives than previously—also admonished the group about the current state insurance regulatory system. He stressed the need for the NAIC to move promptly toward a system of uniformity, saying, "In the meantime, we [Congress] will continue to explore other avenues for reform while working with the states to improve the system from within."

It seemed that the problems had built to a critical mass, and there was now real pressure on the NAIC and the states to create a uniform and fair national system. The NAIC had attempted in late 2002 to create state uniformity by offering states the ability to join a newly adopted "interstate insurance compact" that covered certain limited areas (life, disability, long-term care, and annuities). However, because the NAIC had no statutory enforcement power, it could not force a state uniformity agreement, and the interstate compact was not adopted by all the states.

Still, the urgent call for uniformity from both within and without the NAIC was something new. For the first time, the NAIC was discussing the problem and contemplating change. The word at the NAIC meeting seemed to be "create uniformity or else." For years, few in the insurance industry would criticize the McCarran-Ferguson Act. This was no longer the case.

Dramatically underscoring the turnaround at the end of 2003, the incoming NAIC president, Ernest Csiszar, director of insurance for South Carolina, told the *New York Times* that the NAIC would try to work with Congress, rather than continue fighting a losing battle.[1]

Different Groups, Different Suggestions

The move toward federal regulation started in the late 1990s. In December 1998, a number of important insurance industry groups appeared ready to sacrifice the McCarran-Ferguson Act, which for more than fifty years had protected the states' right to legislate the insurance business. The groups included the American Insurance Association (AIA), the leading property and casualty trade organization in the United States; the National Association of Mutual Insurance Companies (NAMIC); and, to some extent, the National Association of Independent Insurers (NAII).[2]

The AIA represents more than 300 insurance companies, which in 1998 wrote more than $60 billion in premiums annually. That year, the AIA created a special committee of its board of directors charged with undertaking an internal review of the adequacy of current insurance regulation. The AIA identified many areas in which a federal system, if implemented properly, could be preferable to the current state regulatory system.[3,4] In 2007, the AIA remained in the forefront of those associations favoring a federal system of regulation. It supported the legislation introduced in 2006 and 2007 by Senators Tim Johnson (D, South Dakota) and John Sununu, Jr. (R, New Hampshire) calling for an optional federal charter, which would allow the insurance companies to decide whether they want to be regulated by the state or federal government.

The American Council of Life Insurance (ACLI) has also consistently favored federal regulation. In 2007, the ACLI—headed by Frank Keating, the former governor of Oklahoma—released a study saying that by switching to a federal system, life insurers would save $5.7 billion per year.[4] The study also noted other potential benefits, including increased competition and improved speed-to-market for new products.

The ACLI had studied the industry in 1998. According to that study, among the advantages of a federal regulatory scheme were uniformity and faster regulatory approvals. The ACLI realized that for a federal regulatory scheme to work, it must be good for all segments of the insurance industry, not just the life insurers.[5] The study also pointed to drawbacks. For example, the property-casualty business, a rate-regulated industry, could be adversely affected if, for example, one heavy-handed federal rate regulator could suppress property casualty rates. Nevertheless, the group concluded that federal regulation would help the entire industry. The ACLI still holds this viewpoint.[5] Another novel approach put forth in the late 1990s came from the American Bankers Association Insurance Association (ABAIA). The group recommended the creation of a dual chartering system, similar to what has prevailed in the banking business for more than 130 years. Industry observers thought that such a system had problems and needed further study.[6] The ABAIA prepared draft legislation on such a system and submitted it to Congress. In 2007, the dual chartering system in the form of an optional federal charter was being seriously discussed.

Best's Review, a monthly insurance news magazine, became critical of the state regulatory system in the late 1990s. For example, a January 1999 article in *Best's* made ten predictions pointing to change in the insurance industry "on a scale never before seen. What's ahead is change and more change—at an accelerating rate."[7]

Best's also surveyed insurers, brokers, state and federal regulators, and insurance regulators and concluded that state insurance regulation was not keeping up with the rapid changes affecting the industry. The *Best's* survey showed, not surprisingly, that the group with the highest regard for the current regulatory system was the state regulators themselves. Those surveyed were not sure that federal regulation was the answer to the industry's problems. The survey did not offer solutions. It merely measured perceptions of important constituencies about the way the industry was regulated. However, the survey's prevailing sentiment appeared to be that the current state system was not advanced enough, uniform enough, proactive, or innovative enough.[8]

One of the major projections made by *Best's* in 1999 was that Supreme Court decisions, market forces, and the merger of Citigroup with Travelers Insurance "will force regulatory reform within five . . . years."[9] Although this and other predictions did not occur in the next five years, market forces have now formed, pushing for the regulatory reform and federal oversight that *Best's* predicted.

In 2007, *Best's* continued to report on national and international pressures in the insurance market and to predict a legislative solution to chart the industry's future course.

Dual State-Federal Chartering and Oversight

In June 1999, the American Enterprise Institute (AEI) for Public Policy Research held a unique conference on the subject of optional federal chartering and regulation of insurance companies.[10] AEI's Peter J. Wallison observed that unlike calls for change in the past, this time the interest in federal chartering had welled up from within the industry itself. The AEI noted that "by 1999 there was a substantial body of industry opinion favoring optional federal chartering," which arose out of two concerns: (1) costs and competitive handicaps that arise in a multistate regulatory environment, and (2) the intrusiveness and pervasiveness of regulation, especially rate regulation, at the state level.

Wallison further noted an interesting anomaly: that while it was difficult to find advocates for federal chartering and regulation, that was "not necessarily because the case [for federal chartering and regulation] is weak or unpopular, but because individual insurance companies were reluctant to step forward as advocates when such a step could incur the displeasure of their current state regulators."[11]

Impact of Converting to a Federal System

Professors Martin F. Grace and Robert W. Klein of the Center for Risk Management and Insurance Research at Georgia State University performed a study to determine what impact the change from state to federal regulation of the insurance industry would have. They found a $4.5 billion annual savings in converting to a federal system, and that optional federal chartering or other structural changes could promote better regulatory policies.[12]

Furthermore, the professors observed that if a federal agency with a uniform set of regulations regulated the market, there could be a significant reduction in the number of rates and forms and regulatory personnel as well as expenditures. They further noted that there was little doubt that a state-based regulatory system significantly increases insurers' regulatory compliance costs and costs for license applications, among other expenses. They also believed that federal regulation might reduce insurer insolvency costs.

Although states have been roundly criticized for not responding quickly or effectively enough to consumers, Grace and Klein believed that the greatest advantage to keeping state regulation may be in the responsiveness of state regulatory personnel in addressing complaints and providing other consumer services. According to the professors, the need to develop effective and efficient regulatory policies was clear.[13] Today, that need has not changed.

Industry Position on Federal Regulation

Some insurance carriers, such as AIG, have spoken out directly in favor of a federal charter option for property and casualty companies, but only for commercial lines business. AIG recommended preserving state regulation in the noncommercial lines business.

AIG noted that life insurers are much more readily accepting of the federal notion because life insurance is a less location-specific issue. AIG recommended that if a federal insurance system were to be implemented, the Federal Reserve should supervise it, since it is considered a truly independent agency of the federal government.

The insurer cautioned that there are state sensitivities to contend with, among them that state insurance departments are a source of employment, part of the power structure, and a source of tax revenue for the state. Nevertheless, AIG believed that, where necessary, federal law should preempt state law so that state laws do not frustrate the efficient operation of insurance companies.[14]

The Council of Life Insurance Agents & Brokers also favored a federal option, at least as a spur to state action to make existing laws more uniform. In doing so, the Council raised a serious question about whether the McCarran-Ferguson Act remains either relevant or necessary in a world where the financial services industry in general (and the insurance industry in particular) has become national in scope, or where World Trade Organization agreements are on the verge of creating fully developed global markets. The Council further opined that:

> It has become increasingly apparent from our perspective, that the policy objectives embodied in the McCarran-Ferguson Act are questionable in the context of an increasingly internationalized insurance world. . . . McCarran thus serves no functional purpose beyond adding millions of dollars in unnecessary administrative costs. . . . [T]he time is long past due for seriously considering the

manner in which McCarran should be updated to reflect those changes.[15]

Thus, while major insurers, insurance industry associations, and trade journals have seen the need for creating a federal role, opinions vary on what the shape of that role should be.

Consumer Position on Federal Regulation

Robert Hunter, the director of the Consumer Federation of America (CFA), cited major international merger trends and trade agreements, strain at the state level, the sale of insurance on the Internet, the impact of the Gramm-Leach-Bliley Act (which broke down the walls between banks, insurance, and brokers), and competition among states to attract insurance providers as reasons a federal role in the insurance industry was needed. Hunter urged the government not to rush to judgment, and recommended a one-year study of both the policies underlying the McCarran-Ferguson Act and what, in today's economic climate, the appropriate federal role should be.[16]

Hunter stopped just short of endorsing a federal option, pending the study, and cautioned that federal regulation might not be the total answer. He cited the federal government's past regulatory failures (for example, with the Savings and Loan industry) and current problems with ERISA. Despite such problems, the CFA agreed that the current state regulatory system, especially in the area of consumer protection, was not working properly and probably cannot be fixed; for this reason, the CFA appeared to be leaning toward a federal insurance law. Still, the group remained mindful of the bureaucratic and sometimes one-size-fits-all nature of federal government regulation, which it would support only if it was convinced that federal regulation would truly protect the consumer.[17]

Congressional Response to the Insurance Industry Crisis

The U.S. Congress is awakening to the serious problems of the industry and the need for federal laws to govern insurance. There has been a flurry of activity in recent years, starting in 2001 and continuing each year to the present. Different bills with different ideas were introduced but none has yet passed.

On December 21, 2001, Senator Charles Schumer (D, New York), with drafting help from the ABAIA, introduced a far-reaching and comprehensive bill requiring a federal presence in governing the insurance industry. The Schumer bill, entitled the National Insurance Chartering and Supervision Act (NICSA), covered not only the creation of optional federal chartering but also the issues of solvency, audits, reinsurance, consumer protection, and criminal penalties for fraud. In 2002, Representative John J. LaFalce (D, New York) introduced H.R. 3766, the Insurance Industry Modernization and Consumer Protection Act. Like Schumer's bill, it was an effort to create a comprehensive federal law governing insurance.

Beth L. Climo, executive director of the ABAIA, applauded Schumer's bill, saying, "In light of the recent terrorist attacks it is clearer now than ever before: the insurance industry is a national business that affects all aspects of our economy and in a post Gramm-Leach-Bliley marketplace, the federal government needs to expand its understanding of this business." Climo added that Schumer's legislation provided "a terrific foundation for hearings and moving legislation on this very important subject."[18]

Both LaFalce's and Schumer's bills call for an optional dual chartering system, similar to the U.S. banking system (where there is state or federal regulation, depending on whether a state or federal charter is applied for). However, in my view, a dual chartering insurance system may not be the answer to the issues facing the complex insurance industry. Congress may realize that while all of the issues identified in the LaFalce and Schumer bills are important and Congress should address them, the ultimate issue—that of who controls the industry, the states or the federal government—should resolve itself in favor of the federal government.

The move toward accepting federal oversight of the insurance industry continues to gain momentum. In 2002, observers noted that approximately 40 percent of insurance industry executives favored federal oversight and regulation of the insurance industry, and a former insurance commissioner remarked that we are "inching closer to a federal law controlling the industry."[19] In December 2003, the *New York Times* reported that executives at some of the nation's largest insurance companies were lobbying for the creation of a single federal regulator to replace the current system of state-by-state insurance regulation. It was reported that the proposal was gaining ground in Congress.[20]

In 2003, Senator Ernest F. Hollings (D, South Carolina) introduced legislation to create even stronger federal oversight than provided in either the Schumer or La Falce bills, as well as a federal regulator. Some of the key elements of Hollings's bill (known as the Insurance Consumer Protection Act of 2003, S. 1373) included creating a Federal Insurance Commission in the Department of Commerce with responsibilities for licensing and standards, regulation of rates and policies, annual examination and solvency review, investigation of market conduct, and the establishment of accounting standards.

The Hollings bill also proposed allowing intrastate insurers (insurance companies doing business only in the state in which they are domiciled) to remain regulated by states; interstate insurers would be regulated by the federal commission. The bill also proposed creating an independent office of consumer protection, putting enforcement in the hands of the Department of Justice, and creating a national guaranty corporation to pay claims in the event of insolvency. The concepts in the Hollings bill were endorsed by the CFA.

In November 2004, after New York Attorney General Eliot Spitzer lodged bid-rigging charges against major players in the insurance industry, Senator Peter Fitzgerald (R, Illinois), the chair of the Governmental Affairs Subcommittee on Federal Financial Management, Government Information, Federal Services, and International Security, held the first congressional hearing on the issues surrounding the allegations of insurance fraud. Noted industry spokespersons testified about a litany of problems with the state-regulated industry. Fitzgerald declared that it might be time to get the federal government involved in regulating the insurance industry, and to have Congress consider repealing the McCarran-Ferguson Act, especially the antitrust exemption. He believed that having a federal presence would allow the federal government to perform its time-honored role "that guarantees competition and fights the mischief of undue market concentration." The tenor of Congress had clearly changed.

In late 2004 and early 2005, Ohio Representative Oxley, teaming with Representative Richard Baker (R, Louisiana), proposed the SMART bill (State Modernization and Regulatory Transparency Act), which would create a council of federal and state officials to oversee insurance nationally, with a presidential appointee as its head. It would attempt to push the states to adopt uniform standards and would permit the market to determine insurance prices (a form of deregulation), rather than have them determined or approved by regulators, as the states generally do now. The federal umbrella, to be known as a State-National Partnership, would be an advisory body that would try to achieve uniformity among the states, but it would not have any enforcement power.

The House Financial Services Committee held hearings on the SMART bill in front of a packed audience in June 2005. The bill was criticized by both the regulatory and consumer sides. Diane Koken (the Pennsylvania insurance commissioner and the NAIC's 2005 president) and Robert Hunter of the CFA, for example, both opposed the bill.

Criticism of the SMART bill focused on the potential confusion resulting from the split authority of federal and state regulators, as well as the perceived diminution of current state consumer protections, including the elimination of government oversight and approval of rates and rate increases. The bill was sent back to the congressional staff for review. Trade observers felt that until these issues were resolved, the prospects for passage of SMART remained uncertain. After the hearings, a pared-down version of the bill, dubbed SMART-Lite, was introduced. It had significantly fewer provisions than the original.

In April 2006, another attempt was made to overhaul the insurance industry's regulatory problems. The National Insurance Act of 2006, S. 2509, was introduced in the Senate by John Sununu of New Hampshire and Tim Johnson of South Dakota. The bill would allow insurers a choice of a federal or state charter. An Office of National Insurance would be created as an independent office within the Treasury Department, with a presidential appointee as commissioner. The commissioner would have strong oversight, rule-making, and enforcement power. Within the Office of National Insurance would be a Division of Consumer Protection and a Division of Insurance Fraud. Committing a fraudulent insurance act would become a federal crime. The national office would set uniform standards for all insurers holding a federal charter, but would let the marketplace dictate insurance rates. States would continue to regulate only those insurers that opted to operate under a state charter.

In discussing why Congress ought to pass the bill, Sununu said, "State commissioners may have hoped to achieve uniformity and market-based reform within the state regulatory scheme, but those improvements have simply not occurred and are not expected in the near future." A similar bill was introduced in the House.

In June 2006, a subcommittee of the Senate Judiciary Committee held a hearing on the implications of repealing the McCarran-Ferguson Act. At the hearing, a strong panel of industry spokespersons and association heads urged its repeal. The American Bar Association also testified in favor of repeal of the antitrust exemption granted to insurers by the act.[21]

In July 2006, the Senate Committee on Banking, Housing, and

Urban Affairs held hearings to discuss the insurance reform legislation concepts in Sununu and Johnson's National Insurance Act. The act failed to be voted out of committee. In 2007, Sununu and Johnson reintroduced the bill, and a companion bill was introduced in the House by Representative Ed Royce (R, California). In light of the spotlight put on the insurance industry by recent events, including the Spitzer investigations and the Katrina denial of claims, the bill received much scrutiny.

Also in 2007, the Insurance Industry Competition Act was introduced in the Senate by Senator Patrick Leahy (D, Vermont), chair of the Judiciary Committee; Senator Arlen Specter (R, Pennsylvania), the ranking committee member; and others. The act would repeal the McCarran-Ferguson Act and the favored antitrust exemptions granted to the insurance industry. A similar bill was introduced in the House. A bipartisan group of senators and representatives expressed concern about the way insurance companies were handling this important part of the economy, and indicated that they saw no need for the antitrust exemption to continue.

Some observers praised this legislation as exemplifying Congress's new understanding of the problems, and a step toward revamping the regulatory scheme. Others have seen this as a knee-jerk reaction and an attempt to punish the industry for its poor performance in handling Hurricane Katrina claims. Still others noted that the legislators failed to address the other key problem with McCarran-Ferguson: the lack of federal oversight of the insurance industry.

This was not the first time that there was a flurry of activity in Congress to change the insurance industry. In the 1980s, Representative Jack Brooks (D, Texas) introduced legislation, only to see it fail to get out of committee. In the 1990s, Representative John Dingell, Jr. (D, Michigan) introduced legislation to reform the industry, but that too failed. However, at the time those bills were introduced, the industry and the country were not faced with the international, consumer, and other problems that currently exist.

At this writing, it is not known how well the current bills will do in Congress, once the committee hearings and revision sessions begin. However, the concept of federal oversight finally seems to have caught on. If bills are voted out of committee, there is sure to be significant debate over the myriad issues they raise.

Regulatory research groups—even those favoring free enterprise and limited government, such as the Competitive Enterprise Institute (CEI)—agree that the insurance landscape has changed. The CEI's January 2005 report "Federal Insurance Chartering—The Devil's in the Details," by Catherine England, noted a shift in thinking among many in the industry. In the report, England posits the concept of federal insurance chartering, with a federal regulator at the helm, as a real possibility, and she discusses the pros and cons.

Where Insurance Regulation Stands Today

The NAIC desires an interstate compact to create uniformity. Many in Congress (including Schumer and LaFalce) are pushing for an Optional Federal Charter, a dual regulatory system similar to the state and federal banking system. Others, such as proponents of the SMART bill (Baker, Oxley, and others), want to keep the state system, but also want to create a federal-state advisory partnership to provide uniformity and to deregulate. Some (such as former Senator Hollings) have proposed a sole federal regulator. Other suggestions, permutations, and proposals are no doubt in the offing.

It is clear that the insurance issue has now been raised front and center, and Congress seems intent on passing a new law. Many of the reforms proposed over the past few years are still sitting on the shelf or in committee or are in different stages of review, but none of these new legislative ideas has been voted out of committee or brought up for a vote. More legislation will be proposed, but so far, there has been no change in the insurance system.

A New Uniform Federal Omnibus Insurance Law (UFOIL)

As the insurance industry grapples with the tough issues, the movement has been toward some type of federal regulation of the insurance industry. This is not to say that federal regulation will be the total answer. On balance, however, it is clear that there are so many problems with the present state insurance regulatory system that a serious look at the viability of implementing a uniform federal insurance system is needed immediately.

Assessing the Options

Here are some of the options that have been suggested:

1. Leaving the state system as is and doing some patchwork repair
2. Creating a truly uniform state system by having all the states adopt a uniform model insurance law
3. Creating an optional dual chartering and supervisory system (federal and state)
4. Passing a new Uniform Federal Omnibus Insurance Law (UFOIL)

Option 1: Keeping the Status Quo

History has shown that the states are simply not capable of working together in the insurance arena, notwithstanding the good auspices and intentions of the NAIC. Because of budgetary constraints or other reasons, many of the state insurance commissioners are either unwilling or unable to properly enforce their own insurance laws and carry out the intent of the citizens.

In addition, many industry leaders recognize the serious limitations of the present system. The states cannot handle the impact of globalization, the Internet, insurance officer accountability problems, and audit vigilance, among other issues. Problems such as these are much better solved by the federal government—in this case, by creating a uniform set of laws for this growing sector of the economy.

Those who wish to keep the state regulatory system argue that the individual states, especially in the property and casualty insurance area, need latitude to address their specific state and regional problems, for example, the larger need for terrorism insurance regulation in New York and the larger need for farm insurance regulation in the Midwest. Those arguing for a federal system point to the need for a single uniform regulatory scheme. They say that while there are a few specific state and regional issues, the individual states could easily add specific insurance regulatory legislation to a uniform standard base to address those regional issues. They cite other state legislative add-ons, such as in the federally regulated areas of agriculture, banking, environment, health, and transportation, where states have added their own statutes and regulations on top of the federal standards. They can do the same in the area of insurance.

Option 2: Creating a Model Law for All States to Adopt

This is a laudable idea, but it is probably not achievable. It requires that all the states agree to create and live by a truly uniform set of rules. The NAIC or some other organization could draft the model law, which would incorporate the best features of the various state insurance laws into one uniform code. The law would be administered and enforced in a fair and uniform manner in every state by a super-body state overseer and by the courts. The overseer could be the NAIC or a similar agency.

To be effective, the law would have to be promptly adopted by every state legislature, which is unlikely—especially since, if there were any amendments or changes, they too would have to be approved by all the states. Political and historical realism dictates that an agreement adopted by all fifty states is highly unlikely; if it did happen, it would take decades to implement. Thus, this alternative probably would fail of its own weight. Similar efforts—for example, to get all the states to adopt an interstate compact for life insurance companies, pursuant to the Gramm-Leach-Bliley Act of 1999—have failed. Yet there are those who cling to the belief that the states are ready to adopt a uniform model law.

Option 3: Creating an Optional Dual Federal and State Regulatory System

This option is similar to what has existed in the U.S. banking system for approximately 130 years, where there are state and federal banking institutions. Insurers would be given the choice of being regulated by a state or federal body of law.

The most recent regulatory reform bill before Congress falls into this category, calling for the creation of an optional federal charter (OFC).[22] This is a hybrid concept that moves control away from the states but does not give it solely to the federal government. Critics point out that in the banking industry, state regulators oversee only state-chartered institutions, and federal regulators handle only federally chartered institutions. There is a clear delineation between the two regulatory bodies and the different institutions they regulate.

In my opinion, dual chartering of the insurance industry would be too cumbersome to handle the complex structures of insurance companies, where there is more overlap than in banking, and, therefore, not that easily differentiated.

Option 4: Creating a Uniform Federal Omnibus Insurance Law (UFOIL)

This option may be the most sweeping, but it also makes the most sense. UFOIL could incorporate the best of the current state insurance laws and state insurance departments' regulations. In addition, the best of the industry associations, such as the NAIC, would have a strong oversight role and, to the greatest extent possible, the current revenue stream for each state and the rights of the consumer would be preserved.

The federal government would set the rules and standards and would delegate enforcement to the state agency (with assistance of an industry association, if necessary), and that state agency would then carry out the rules and standards. All states would be held to a minimum federal standard, but states could add additional language to handle contentious local and region-specific issues.

Over time, if managed properly, UFOIL could drastically cut costs to the consumer and the industry, allowing for the creation of a less expensive insurance product with greater coverage. It could create a fairer and more uniform claim process, as well as a more predictable regulatory and cost structure, which would significantly reduce most consumers' insurance premiums.

The first step toward UFOIL is a government study of the insurance industry, leading to recommendations. Assuming the study confirms the need for a federal system, comprehensive input from the industry and the public would be solicited, which would lead to the drafting and passage of UFOIL.

While it is important to move as quickly as we can, the law must be carefully drafted and implemented, with fairness to industry and consumer alike. It also should be remembered that insurance is really a national marketplace, with certain regional problems, and therefore regulatory rule making should be based on a national market, with states assisting in drafting language to cover the local and regional issues.

Think how much simpler, more efficient, and less costly the delivery of the insurance product in the United States would be if we created one uniform federal standard, with individual states having the right to add regional specifics if needed. Under a federal UFOIL law, the states, as deputies, could act as the local eyes and ears providing the federal government with an early warning system, and thereby giving the uniform federal regulatory system enough time to anticipate, analyze, and solve issues, before they become major problems.

The options are on the table. We need to act.

Notes

1. Joseph B. Treaster, "Consumer Groups Criticize Insurance Regulations Chief," *New York Times* Section C; col. 5, Business/Financial Desk, p. 10, March 4, 2004, quoting Ernest Csisar in 2003, incoming President of the NAIC for 2004.
2. Editorial, Underwriters Report, Inc., December 10, 1998.
3. American Insurance Association officials, January 1999.
4. Steven W. Pottier, "State Regulation of Life Insurers: Implications for Economic Efficiency and Financial Strength," ACLI study, May 30, 2007.
5. Pottier, "State Regulation of Life Insurers."
6. "This regulatory proposal merits serious consideration," *National Underwriter* (Life/Health/FinancialServices), October 25, 1999.
7. "An Emerging New Landscape," *Best's Review*, Property/Casualty Edition, January 1999.
8. Etti G. Baranoff and Daniel Gattis, "Measuring Attitudes toward Regulation," *Best's Review*, Property/Casualty Edition, September 1998.
9. "An Emerging New Landscape."
10. Peter J. Wallison, ed., *Optional Federal Chartering and Regulation of Insurance Companies* (Washington, D.C.: AEI Press, 2000). The American Enterprise Institute for Public Policy Research was the first policy research organization to give extended conference exposure to the question of federal regulation of the insurance industry, an idea that had been the subject of considerable interest in the insurance industry for many years. The conference took place in June 1999, and submissions came from major organizations and insurers stating their perspective on the issue. It should be noted that the conference was held before the passage of the Gramm-Leach-Bliley Act.
11. Wallison, "Introduction," in Wallison, *Optional Federal Chartering and Regulation of Insurance Companies.*

12. Martin F. Grace and Robert W. Klein, "Efficiency Implications of Alternative Regulatory Structures," Georgia State University, 2000.

13. Professors Grace and Klein, in Wallison, *Optional Federal Chartering and Regulation of Insurance Companies.*

14. Ernest T. Patrikis, "Optional Federal Chartering for Property and Casualty Companies," in Wallison, *Optional Federal Chartering and Regulation of Insurance Companies.*

15. Joel Wood, "Broker Organizations," in Wallison, *Optional Federal Chartering and Regulation of Insurance Companies.*

16. J. Robert Hunter, "A Consumer Perspective," in Wallison, *Optional Federal Chartering and Regulation of Insurance Companies.* See also testimony of Hunter before the House Committee on Financial Services, Subcommittee on Capital Markets, Insurance, and Government Sponsored Enterprises, "Working with State Regulators to Increase Insurance Choices for Consumers," March 31, 2004.

17. Hunter, "A Consumer Perspective," in Wallison, *Optional Federal Chartering and Regulation of Insurance Companies.*

18. Beth L. Climo, ABIA Executive Director, December 21, 2001.

19. Author interviews with E. Grace Vandecruze, CPA, senior vice president of Fox-Pitt, Kelton, Inc., April 2, 2002, and Linda Kaiser, former Pennsylvania insurance commissioner, April 2, 2002.

20. Joseph B. Treaster, "Insurers Want One Regulator Instead of 50," *New York Times*, December 26, 2003.

21. Donald C. Klawiter, chair of the Antitrust Law Section of the American Bar Association, testimony before the Senate Judiciary Committee urging repeal of the antitrust provisions of the McCarran-Ferguson Act and the establishment of "safe harbors" for certain insurance transactions, June 20, 2006.

22. See National Insurance Act of 2007.

CHAPTER 10

The Solution

UFOIL—A Two-Step Process of Consumerization and Federalization

"We can't expect to win the hearts and minds of public policymakers or consumers simply by spouting statistics that tell folks how many claims we've paid. That type of jargon goes right over most folks' heads when consumers are struggling to afford our products and they perceive that all the private companies have taken their record profits and fled for higher ground. . . ."

> —Joseph Anotti, Property Casualty Insurers Association of America, September 5, 2007

"Federal oversight would provide confidence that the industry is not engaging in the most egregious forms of anticompetitive conduct – price fixing, agreements not to pay, and market allocations."

> —Senator Patrick Leahy (D-Vt.), Chairman, Senate Judiciary Committee, February 15, 2007

"Too many consumers are paying too much for insurance due to the collusive atmosphere that exists in the insurance industry."

> —Senator Arlen Specter (R-Penn.), Ranking Member, Senate Judiciary Committee, February 15, 2007

A Two-Step Process

The problems in the state-regulated insurance industry will only expand and worsen, making the need for federal regulation and oversight imperative. After studying the available options, the only real way to eliminate the vulture culture and the minefield that characterize today's insurance industry is to change the way the industry is regulated and overseen. I therefore urge the creation of a Uniform Federal Omnibus Insurance Law (UFOIL). This requires a two-step process, the first being consumerization (making state regulators more responsive to consumers) and the second being federalization. If this is accomplished, insurance can become a fair and balanced product, uniformly governed, efficiently administered, and reasonably priced.

Step 1: Consumerization

Consumerizing the state insurance departments is practical and quickly doable. As we have seen, many state insurance department officials simply protect the insurance industry—stacking the deck against the consumer. Large numbers of consumer complaints go unresolved, and thousands of new civil lawsuits are filed against insurers each year, some seeking punitive and bad faith damages. Unfortunately, many if not most of these complaints, inquiries, and lawsuits remain unresolved, and some take years to conclude.

By truly consumerizing insurance—not just giving lip service to it—the states would become more responsive to the consumer. More openness, or transparency, into the workings of insurance departments and insurance companies is needed. This can be done by the following:

- Establishing a pro-consumer regulatory environment, with more direct interface and outreach to the public

- Implementing an independent Office of Insurance Consumer Advocate, or a strong office of insurance consumer services within each insurance department, dedicated to being the voice and legal arm of the consumer in each state

- Educating the consumer as to insurance availability, rate and benefit comparisons, understanding policy language, and claims processing

- Carefully scrutinizing insurers' requests for rate increases and policy language approval

- Performing better oversight into insurer claims handling and market conduct

- Monitoring insurance executives' behavior and the solvency of insurers

Included in effective consumerization is the need to emphasize the new reality of judicial punishment for the fraudulent claimant. The public must be made more aware of the serious consequences of frivolous lawsuits and exaggerated claims. The state needs to demonstrate to the fraudulent claimant and his or her representatives that there are significant individual civil and criminal penalties for such activities and that the laws will be enforced.

Consumerization can effectively be achieved in each state at a relatively small cost and within a fairly short amount of time. The positive action of an effective and committed state insurance commissioner, strong insurance department deputies, knowledgeable consumers, a consumer-friendly legislature, an attorney general's office committed to enforcing the laws, and a proactive state governor would go a long way toward achieving these goals.

Step 2: Federalization

The second step—federalization of regulation and oversight of the insurance industry—is more complex and therefore will take more time. But it is achievable.

Federalization, the direct regulatory power and oversight by the federal government, involves a four-phase process:

1. An immediate independent federal study of the insurance industry by a blue-ribbon panel
2. The repeal or significant modification and update of the McCarran-Ferguson Act of 1945
3. The passage of a Uniform Federal Omnibus Insurance Law (UFOIL) and publication of rules in the Code of Federal Regulations (CFR), which would provide the basis for federal regulation
4. The creation of a position of Federal Insurance Regulator, through a Federal Insurance Administration, which could be a cabinet-level position of Secretary of Insurance or a Department of Insurance within the Treasury Department

A Call for the Passage of a Federal Law

To create uniformity of law and efficiency in the administration of the insurance product in the United States, I propose that Congress draft and pass a Uniform Federal Omnibus Insurance Law, which would create a single federal agency responsible for chartering and supervising the industry. The states and some associations would function as deputies under the federal umbrella. The new UFOIL would:

- Establish a federal floor for uniform insurance standards and allow each state to build additional protections for the consumer and the insurer as each state deems warranted.

- Require the federal government to provide administration and oversight, but also preserve many of the current functions of the state insurance departments.

- Be based on the theory of delegation of powers to the states, and, therefore, would not create redundancies. Under our federal system and Constitution, a structure is in place for the states to act as deputies to carry out federal law. The idea of the federal government deputizing the states is not new. In fact, states already perform the administrative and enforcement functions of federal law in a number of areas. What would be new insofar as the insurance industry is concerned is the uniformity of policy approval, marketing, licensing, market conduct review, claims administration and adjudication, audits, reserves, and solvency. Also new would be the decreased cost of regulatory compliance to the insurers.

- Use the services of important insurance industry associations (such as the NAIC) to act as additional empowered representatives and to submit policy recommendations.

- Preserve the same or similar tax revenues for each of the states (adjusting as necessary for changed circumstances).

- Be revenue-neutral and not create any new burdens on taxpayers.

- Take the best of the states' insurance laws and mold them into a coherent and uniform federal statute. It would allow some realistic adjustments for local or regional rate, regulatory, underwriting, or claims handling issues (such as high-rise residential and office building coverage in urban areas, farm issues in rural areas, and hurricane coverage in areas prone to adverse weather conditions).

If structured properly, UFOIL could streamline the delivery of insurance products with a minimum amount of bureaucracy and a significant reduction in cost to both insurer and policyholder. The bottom line is that for the average insurance consumer, premiums should be much lower as a result of efficiencies of scale and a uniform system.

Legislative Framework for the Uniform Federal Omnibus Insurance Law

UFOIL should cover important national as well as regional and statewide insurance issues. Properly drafted UFOIL legislation would enumerate such things as:

- Powers of the federal regulator, allowing deputizing of state agencies and national associations to carry out federal law.

- Federal standards, including the right of the states to add to standards and make exceptions to federal standards.

- Powers of a licensed insurer through a federal charter.

- Regulation of agencies and agents.

- Financial regulation of insurers and proper reporting, audit, and solvency requirements.

- Consumer protection regulation and the establishment of a National Consumer Advocate.

- Product regulation: policy standards, filing, rate regulation, market conduct examinations, and so on.

- Examination of and reporting requirements for insurers.

- Enforcement powers, court jurisdiction, and expedited dispute resolution, as well as strong civil and criminal penalties against corporations, employees, and individual claimants.

- Reinsurance regulation, including solvency requirements.

- Regulation of corporate transactions (control, merger, and demutualization of U.S. insurers as well as of off-shore entities doing business in the United States).

- Revenue-neutral taxation and distribution of revenues to the states.

- Guaranty funds.

- International transaction approvals.

- Application of federal antitrust laws to the insurance industry.

Other subissues that could be addressed in the legislation include:

- The requirement for submission and prior approval of countrywide insurance policies, which can then be sold in all fifty states; any special regional differences in coverage can be applied for.

- A central agency clearinghouse and initial adjudication unit (with administrative law judges) for consumer, broker/agent, and insurance carrier complaints and disputes. (This would act to unclog the court system.)

- The creation of an insurance court with experts in the field.

- The establishment of an active financial solvency audit board, to conduct year-round field audits of insurers.

- The establishment of a properly enforced, escrowed, interest-bearing, earmarked reserve fund system, such as a Federal Insurance Guaranty Corporation, financed by regular assessments on insurance companies.

- The establishment of a national guarantee fund for insolvencies, with proper caps on the guarantee (higher than most caps are currently set).

- The establishment of hard-to-place insurance pools (with all carrier participation) for high-risk insureds who or high-risk industries that cannot get insurance elsewhere.

- Formal oversight and approval of entry, merger, and exit from the insurance business.

- Antitrust regulation of the insurance industry and agency review and power to prevent and prohibit antitrust violations.

- Agency authority to enact binding regulations.

- An investigative civil and criminal enforcement arm, with civil and criminal penalties for violations of the law.

- A system of fees and/or assessments from the insurance companies, brokers/agents, and consumers and augmentation of federal tax and budget dollars to support the federal insurance agency and to distribute a major portion of insurance premium taxes or other revenue to the deputized state insurance departments and associations.

- A system to monitor and report on the impact of the agency and legislation on the consumer public, as well as a periodic program to provide status reports and to recommend changes in the law to the legislative and executive branches of the federal government.

- A public relations department to provide current information to the consumer.

- Delegation of certain powers to the states, as necessary from time to time. The proposed federal insurance agency could have the power to delegate to the states the administration of an "assigned risk pool" in each state, or the agency may require the states to perform other appropriate duties helpful to the administration of the overall insurance program, such as over-sight of claim administration practices on a uniform federal basis. Where necessary, a specific regional or statewide issue could be exempted from federal oversight and be specifically administered by the state.

- Establishment of a healthcare division to oversee the uniform application and delivery of insurance benefits to consumers, as well as to oversee the application and delivery of physical and mental health parity by insurers.

- Civil and criminal accountability for insurance companies and insurance executives, board members, and insurance employ-ees, as well as consumer claimants, who intentionally violate the law.

- A properly staffed and funded Office of Insurance Consumer Advocate section, to take up the consumer cause when war-ranted.

Regulatory Issues

Once UFOIL has passed, a Notice of Proposed Rule Making would be employed to flesh out the regulations. The Secretary of Insurance would be authorized to create rules and standards, and to charter, examine, supervise, and generally regulate and have oversight over those engaged in the business of insurance.

Supervisory standards created by the Secretary of Insurance would include requirements and standards for capital, liquidity, investment, lending, accounting, audit, and valuation. Consumer standards created by the Secretary of Insurance would include consumer advocate representatives, consumer information, consumer privacy, market conduct examinations, advertising, discrimination, claims practices, tie-in sales, and other consumer issues.

Enforcement Rules

A new federal insurance agency will be needed to enforce the changes in the regulatory climate. The Federal Insurance Administration already exists, but this agency is very limited and, while important, at present deals only with flood insurance and other fragmented insurance programs. Congress could simply expand the jurisdiction and power of the Federal Insurance Administration to incorporate comprehensive regulation and supervision of the insurance industry.

The proposed federal insurance agency would be the central clearinghouse and regulator for all major insurance functions, which, if implemented and properly funded, could be a win-win situation for consumers and industry alike. Enforcement could be carried out by deputized state insurance departments or by an association such as the NAIC.

The Need for Bipartisan and Executive Support

There will no doubt be quite a bit of public debate over a new Uniform Federal Omnibus Insurance Law. The issues and concepts as identified here and elsewhere must be studied and implemented in a comprehensive and fair manner, with bipartisan congressional support and a sincere endorsement by the president.

UFOIL will take discussion and thought and will require solicitation of comments, in particular from the insurers and consumers. If enacted, it should be a lasting statutory document, complete with administrative and regulatory oversight and uniform enforceability, all of which will benefit the states, the insurance industry, and the public.

Turning the Tide with UFOIL

A vulture culture has been circling the insurance industry, ready to strike. In many cases, it has struck. That said, it is also important to recognize that insurance is important to our economy. Most insurance serves a vital need, and most of those working in the industry or affected by it are acting ethically and within proper guidelines. Still, the problems are real and the potential for a crisis that could affect the industry and the millions of policyholders and claimants it serves is growing. The good news is that there is still time to take corrective action. We must and we can change the rules under which the insurance industry currently operates.

If, as anticipated, an independent study such as the one proposed concludes that the problems we've examined cannot be corrected in a proper and timely manner within the current system, we must call for more radical change: replacement of the present system of state regulation, administration, and oversight of the insurance industry with a national one where the federal government, and not the states, would create and enforce a uniform set of rules and regulations for the fair protection of the consumer, the insurance industry, and the public.

Transforming the industry through the two-step process of consumerization and federalization described here, and governing it pursuant to a new Uniform Federal Omnibus Insurance Law such as the one proposed, would benefit consumers, the industry, and those who work in it.

The laws and regulations dealing with the insurance industry need to be stronger, uniformly applied, and properly enforced in all states. Stiffer penalties for violations by the industry and consumers are essential.

Under UFOIL, insurance companies should be able to cut regulatory compliance and other costs, have uniform policy form approvals, and operate under a common code of conduct. Brokers and agents would benefit from more streamlined licensing.

UFOIL would serve as a floor for uniform, standardized law and enforcement procedures, and would regularize the receipt of tax revenues from premiums collected in each state, which would benefit states and regulators. To meet local or regional needs, states could build additional laws on top of the floor as long as they did not conflict with the basic concepts of UFOIL.

UFOIL would lead to fairer coverage, eliminate confusion, and give claimants a better understanding of their rights. It would also provide for uniform claim review and enable prompt processing and proper payment. Taxpayers could see reduced taxes as a result of more efficient insurance regulation, which, in turn, could reduce costs to insurers, resulting in a reduction in premiums and premium taxes to the consumer. The judicial system would benefit from fewer lawsuits and more consistent decisions. Politicians and legislators would hear fewer complaints from their constituents and the media.

If there is no change, we may all become victims of the increasing number of major insurance company failures, rogue executives, or unresolved consumer complaints. However, because the public, the claimant, the insurer, and the government now realize that we are all in it together, we have a greater opportunity than at any time in the past to do something to fix the system before it can do greater harm.

We should not let this opportunity slip through our fingers. The insurance system needs to be overhauled, and quickly. Failure to do so could mean that each of us, as individual or business insurance consumers, might be one major contested insurance claim away from a crisis, one major insurance company failure away from financial disaster. If we neglect the insurance regulatory problem, we do so at our peril knowing that it could become a threat to the country's political, social, and economic infrastructure.

The federal government can stop the vulture culture in the insurance industry by passing UFOIL, and we must keep the pressure on our legislators to do so. The federal government can bring back trust to the industry, create uniformity and predictability, and lower costs for consumer and insurer alike.

We must change the rules under which the insurance industry is operating, or accept the vulture culture as the consequence of our inaction. Which will it be? I recommend that we change the rules now and create a Uniform Federal Omnibus Insurance Law. When our nation speaks out and shows its collective will, as it has done many times in the past, change for the better can happen here as well.

It must be done. It can be done.

INDEX

ABOUT THE AUTHOR

Paul Facenda Studios

Eric D. Gerst, Esq., a legal consultant, has practiced law nationwide for more than thirty years, during which time he concentrated in the areas of insurance and transportation. At various times, he represented different sides of the insurance equation: consumers and insurance companies, brokerage firms, and others. He has handled complex litigation for plaintiffs and defendants and has transactional experience in many facets of the insurance business.

In 2003, Pennsylvania Governor Edward G. Rendell appointed Mr. Gerst to his Insurance Transition Committee. The committee was active preceding the governor's inauguration through the first few months of the governor's term of office. The committee presented recommendations to the incoming governor regarding the functioning of the Pennsylvania Insurance Department, including recommendations about the Pennsylvania insurance commissioner, insurance issues facing the Commonwealth of Pennsylvania, and suggested changes. After the Transition Committee fulfilled its duties and was discharged, Mr. Gerst continued to submit position papers, information, and recommendations to the governor, the insurance commissioner, and the governor's Medical Malpractice Task Force.

For many years, Mr. Gerst was senior partner in the law firm Gerst, Heffner, Carpenter and Podgorsky, with offices in Philadelphia and Washington, D.C. While there, he served as outside general counsel to a national insurance brokerage company for almost ten years. In this capacity, he was instrumental in drafting and establishing a new national insurance program for a large sector of the transportation industry at a time when the industry was in crisis and could not obtain reasonably priced insurance, similar to today's medical malpractice insurance situation. During that period, Mr. Gerst gained hands-on familiarity with all aspects of the insurance industry, including each state's different insurance statutes and regulations. He also negotiated extensively with agencies of the state and federal governments on behalf of his clients.

Mr. Gerst has submitted testimony on numerous insurance issues to congressional committees and subcommittees, including the Senate Banking, Housing and Urban Affairs Committee; the House Financial Subcommittee on Housing and Community Opportunity; and the House Financial Services Subcommittee on Capital Markets, Insurance, and Government Sponsored Enterprises. He has also appeared before Senate and House committees on transportation legislation and as counsel on behalf of insurance and transportation clients. He has assisted in formulating federal and state policy and regulations.

In 2005 and 2006, Republicans and Democrats unanimously tapped Mr. Gerst to serve as Judge of Elections in his community, a role demanding broad knowledge of and adherence to state and federal rules. He served as an attorney observer in overseeing critical federal and state elections in 2004 and 2006.

In the summer of 2006, the American Bar Association published advance excerpts from the *Vulture Culture* book in the ABA Insurance Regulation Newsletter as an 8-page Special Feature. In the Fall/ Winter of 2007, the American Bar Association published additional excerpts from the book in the ABA Insurance Regulation Newsletter as a Special Feature.

Mr. Gerst lives in the suburbs of Philadelphia. He is married, with two adult children and a grandchild. He has maintained an active law license since 1968; is a member of the Philadelphia Bar Association, Pennsylvania Bar Association, Washington, D.C. Bar Association, and American Bar Association; and has been admitted to practice before the U.S. Supreme Court. He is a member of the Tort Trial & Insurance Practice Section (TIPS) of the ABA.

You may contact Eric D. Gerst at egerst@gerstlegal.com., or visit his website at www.gerstlegal.com.